FEARLESS THINKING, STRESS-FREE LIVING

- GURANTEED (ALMOST)

A LIFE CHANGING SOLUTION FOR PEACE AND HAPPINESS

PURANDAR A. AMIN

Publisher:
Sapient Advisors, Inc.

P.O. Box 2033, Artesia CA 90701

Publisher: Sapient Advisors, Inc. USA

First Edition

Printed: United State of America

Library of Congress Number: 2017910790

Hard Cover	978-0-9991814-0-9
Trade Paper	978-0-9991814-1-6
Kindle	978-0-9991814-2-3
e-pub	978-0-9991814-3-0
PDF	978-0-9991814-4-7
Audio	978-0-9991814-5-4
Video	978-0-9991814-6-1

Book Layout & eBook conversion by manuscript2ebook.com

DISCLAIMER

The author and publisher disclaim any liability arising out of the use of this book. The reader is advised to seek professional counseling in the medical, spiritual, psychological, and other fields. The information in this book is not all-inclusive and is not applicable to each and every instance without regard to the particular circumstances. No responsibility is assumed for any error or omission, or for any inaccuracy or inconsistency in the information contained in this book. The material contained in this book is educational; therefore, the reader is urged to refer to any other available information on the subject.

DEDICATION

At the lotus feet of Sri Sathya Sai Baba,
For being the divine consciousness personified

Then

Aishwa, Anish, Suhana, Jiana, and Aarav,
All for being infinite expressions of divine consciousness.

GRATITUDE

To all divine personages who gave me direct or indirect blessings
and instructions to illuminate my mind, to radiate
on my intelligence, to correct my actions

To all adversaries who agreed to accept most difficult roles
as my lifelong teachers

To my all near and dear ones who held my hands when I was falling.

To Don Deniston for diligently typing the manuscript,

To Kaitlin Yancey for being my editor,
correcting me again and again.

To Phyllis Hopper for perfecting the final version

To Pankaj Runthala (manuscript2ebook.com),
for providing me his invaluable assistance
in designing and preparing the book for the market

TABLE OF CONTENTS

A NOTE FROM THE AUTHOR

Notice the inclusion of "almost" in the title. I cannot guarantee you a life 100% free of stress because the success of this endeavor also depends upon you. What I am offering are the tools that will help you make a U-turn in your thinking process. These are nothing new, but they seem revolutionary for some people because this type of thinking goes against their conventional wisdom. It will be difficult for you to get benefits of the suggestions here in if you are not willing to set aside your viewpoints, belief systems, and opinions. Since mental conditioning begins at a very early age, these belief systems are deeply ingrained in your very being. Your thought patterns have solidified over time, surrounding you with a strong invisible wall, designed to prevent you from receiving anything that differs from your established world view. The good news is that all you need in order to break through this wall is time and serious intention.

You should not buy this book if you are not ready to try some of the steps, exercises, and belief systems that will be presented. Why waste the money? Buy this book only if you are ready to live a stress-free life, enjoy your full freedom, and entirely follow a different lifestyle. Some of the suggestions in this book may confront traditional religious beliefs, but the entire approach is secular. Give up all dogmas, and make yourself free. I am not here to defend my approach. Take it if it makes sense to you; leave it if it does not appeal to your mind and heart.

As we open this dialogue, a million thoughts are running through my mind. I have been in your shoes; I have walked through the same minefield of transformation. Make no mistake; this process is about demolishing your old life so that you can build up a new one. That is why I have provided so many cautions in this opening note. Know that I am not challenging you to do anything that I have not done myself. I have experienced failure, I have faced difficulties, I have battled with obstructions, and I have been plagued with doubts. But through all this, I have come out on the other side. So take heart, and know that it can be done.

A Note From The Author

When it comes to stress, countless books have been penned. Millions of articles have been written, and thousands of doctors have said their piece. And yet, all their wisdom and insight has largely failed to help modern individuals deal with their worries. However, having achieved stress-free living myself, I am convinced that my approach can help you find peace. My doctor tells me that my heart is as healthy as a child's. My blood pressure is average, and my cholesterol level is normal.

You will notice that the chapters of this book are arranged as personal letters. I have done this for two reasons: First, the attention span of most people is short. Second, the letter format allows me to talk to you directly, offering clear instructions rather than implying them as a third party. I have chosen my wife, Uma, as a reader to represent you. Uma has been a constant companion in this journey of forty-plus years, having seen the peaks and valleys of life. Now, as I am walking along the banks of the river, who could be a better witness than Uma?

Many times, the discussion in these letters may sound abstract. It may even sound boring if you have not allowed time for self-reflection, or if you have not searched for the answers, or have closed your mind. This is a sign that you need to reverse your thinking. If you travel with me on the path, I assure you that you will be travelling the highway to peace. It is in the abstract that peace is found.

Let us begin the journey together. I can assure you that a worry-free life, full of freedom, awaits you.

Purandar

PREFACE

When I walk along the sandy beaches of Santa Monica or across miles and miles of desert in the Middle East, my mind gets lost in a distant past, where time loses its movement. Peace prevails without reason. Timelessness takes me over, transporting me to another era.

My father had a mango farm in the village where we lived. He hired a watchman to protect the mango crop. I remember the watchman lying beneath the trees on the bare dirt of the land, smoking his small earthenware tobacco pipe. He would talk with passersby, never minding the number of hours that passed or whether he happened to be late or early. He was very happy with simple food and a humble place to sleep, content to be under the trees and counting the stars in the Mediterranean sky. He had no desire to be rich, nor did he dream of visiting distant places. It did not bother him that others were wealthier than he, for he found his riches in the musical sounds his feet would make as they walked across the bed of dry mango leaves. He was not ashamed of his torn clothes; his poverty never bothered him because he believed that his life was entirely normal. He was the most transparent man I had ever seen. He respected me, even though I was a child and he was my elder. Humility was second nature to him. His name was Baboo.

And then there was a woman. She had a meager education and was barely able to read or write. Her husband had a very modest income. Yet I remember her as a most contented person. She never asked for new clothes, exotic perfumes, a bigger house, or luxuries of any kind. She did not visit temples, theaters, or concert halls. Nor did she seek fame or fortune. She had no maid, nor any servants to attend her. She awoke each day at four in the morning to grind grain on a hand-operated stone mill to prepare the day's flour. She worked each day until nine in the evening on family chores. She never had a day of vacation or even a simple day off.

She endeavored to instill strict moral values in her children. She did not display any anger toward her husband or complain about her lack of necessities. She never wasted a single penny. She bore all miseries, discomforts, and the indifferent attitudes of others patiently. And when she died, she was peaceful and content. Her family never understood what was the source of such peace and contentment. Neither her husband nor her children ever fully appreciated her for her strength, her virtues, and her quiet peace. She was my mother.

My own story is quite different from those of Baboo and my mother.

I highly valued my education. I left my village to come to the U.S.A. and pursued all kinds of dreams, desires, and joys. After all, my modern thinking led me to believe that this was the path to happiness. Many struggles, several failures, mountainous tensions, and endless activities eventually compelled me to return to my basic virtues – to find peace in the place where I started. Were Baboo or my mother truly extraordinary persons? So much so that even they did not realize it? Did their modest lives hold the key to true happiness?

This book describes my journey to rediscover myself; a journey to find what is most important to me, what the truth is, what is lasting in life, where bliss – not just temporary happiness – resides, and to discover its source. It is my journey toward living a life of peace and gratitude, even in the midst of the hectic modern world. It is a journey to understand how the inner being –thinking patterns, preconceptions, and beliefs – affects the outer being and how to discover the quality of life we deserve while remaining true to our inner values.

How do we begin such a life-changing journey? We need to go to the source of the problem to find what feeds the stress and tensions in our lives. That source is our mind, where fear exists and stress is born. It not an outside event or a person that causes you stress, but your own reaction to such an event or person. Therefore, we need to understand the mind before we can find a solution. This problem becomes complicated when you realize that the source, the cause, of your problems is also the source of your solution – a perfect duality within perceived imperfect conditions.

First, know thyself.

The world says that knowledge is power. However, it is not power until you use it for your own benefit. Knowing yourself is not that difficult if you allow yourself to be criticized within your intimate relationships and to seek insight into the roots of your own behavior. Take stock of your mental abilities, habits, patterns, and weaknesses. Are you usually calm and slow to grow edgy or anxious? Do you have a quick temper? Are your viewpoints rigidly held, or are you persuadable? Do you have a big ego? Do you consider yourself open to new ideas? These are not mere abstract questions, but ways to examine your true personal assets and liabilities.

Take special note of what disturbs you. Notice your likes and dislikes. Examine why you like some people and not others. Think about where you prefer to spend your time and ask yourself why. Start observing what kinds of thoughts come to you when you are alone. Pay attention to what you avoid, and what you embrace. Identify your habits. What kind of shows do you prefer to watch on TV and what books do you read? Even your choice of clothes, colors, housing, and possessions will tell you who you are. Observe yourself. The world we see is a reflection of the original creator. Therefore, (and this may sound strange to you), if you easily find faults in others, you may be surprised to discover that those faults lie within you.

You must prepare yourself. As you walk with me on this journey, you will find yourself challenged to change many of your ideas and viewpoints. We will explore many aspects of the mind. You may find yourself questioning your own preconceived ideas and quite uncomfortable in the process. But in the end, you will be a happier person, so stick with it. Remember, this is not a quick or easy fix. Your problems will not magically disappear. You may not see instant benefits, but after a month or two, you will probably notice subtle changes have taken place within you. Be steadfast in your journey and know that stress-free living is within your grasp.

Let us begin.

Purandar

1

JUST A THOUGHT

July 2, 2012

Dear Uma,

It is virtually impossible to find a human being who is free from worries and fears. In fact, worries, stress, and fears are so common that they are accepted as a normal part of human existence. To expound, let me enumerate some of the fears I know you have:

- Fear of unemployment or losing your income
- Fear of losing your home
- Fear of losing your life's savings or retirement security
- Fear of losing friends or relatives
- Fear of divorce or broken relationships
- Fear of your children's vulnerability
- Fear of losing your reputation

- Fear of losing a lifetime of memories
- Fear of disease or illness
- Fear of an untimely death
- Fear of situations beyond your control

Worries and stress are the children of fears. And fears are simply thoughts. Nobody has seen fear; it is just a thought, an illusion.

Pause for a second before reading further. Bring your fear into your imagination. Look at it. What do you find? Just a thought. It is extremely important to believe and ingrain in your being that this fear is just a thought. It is the imagining of the fear that made you scared and stressed.

Look at these fears. Know them as thoughts – thoughts about the future. They have no real existence, except as thoughts in your mind. At the risk of being redundant, I can only ask you to remember this observation clearly. Spend some time letting it sink into your consciousness. <u>Understand that we are dealing with thoughts of the future and nothing else.</u>

You must consider one more thing, which plays a powerful part in this process: emotion. If the mind is the subject of the brain, then emotion is the subject of the heart. The combination of thought and emotion can be a deadly poison or a sweet nectar, depending on its nature. For instance, together they can create health problems and pain that affect your body. Here's something to try: The next time you are alone, attempt to find where your thoughts come from, just for fun. As soon as you try to catch them or even look at them, they will disappear. You will find it impossible to trace their root.

Try this now: Hold one particular thought in your awareness as long as you can. You will notice that, while the first thought was trying to escape from you, a second thought was ready to jump in. You will discover that there is a connection of some sort between these two thoughts (although such connections may be difficult for you to identify). This is due to the magnetic properties of thoughts. One worried thought can create a chain of worried thoughts that are unending, ultimately throwing you into a chasm of worries and fears. You must break this automatic thinking machine. We live in an ocean of thoughts, just as fish live in an ocean of water. You need to swim out of it.

Observing your thoughts is the first requirement in our process. As you practice the above exercise, note what happens when you finally look at your thoughts. They will disappear, and you will experience a moment of peace. Try to hold on to that moment of peace for as long as you can. See how easy it is? And we have only just begun!

With Peace,

Purandar

Exercise

For one month, watch your thoughts four times a day when you are alone. Do this for a minute at a time. Write your observations here or in the "My Notes" section.

My Notes

2

MIND

January 27, 2012

Dear Uma,

On this early winter morning, the air is cool and calm. I want to hold it in my hand, as though it were a precious diamond, but alas, except for this feeling, I am empty handed. Oh! I can't live without it, but I'm unable to grab it. So is the mind.

Millions of words have been spoken and written on the subject of the mind. I dare to add my two-cents in hopes that, upon the completion of my discussion, you will view the mind differently. Psychologists and psychiatrists may not agree with what you are going to learn herein, as science lacks the tools necessary to comprehend the precise functioning of the mind. Many confuse the brain with the mind. The brain is just a physical instrument with which we process thoughts (e.g., to bring them into our awareness). The infinite ability of the mind makes it difficult to define within finite parameters. To most people, the mind is a bundle of thoughts. But it is much more than that.

At the most abstract level, the mind is consciousness expressed. This expression is in the form of a thought. Since its roots are in consciousness, a thought possesses the attributes of consciousness. These attributes include components such as energy, light, and magnetism. It is also infinite, creative, and reflective. The mind has an unlimited ability for retention, which makes it a storehouse of memories. And, although science has not discovered it, the mind is also a material of a different kind that can be objectified. The proof? Everything you see with your beautiful eyes was previously a thought – just like water turned into ice.

The mind's form is light – a reflective light. It is reflective because it is not the original source. Because of this, the reflection will disappear if the originating source is removed or changed. If the source light is withdrawn, the mind can disappear. Though this sounds like a very theoretical discussion, this idea and its practice are crucial to removing stress or unhappiness. We will continue to explore this concept later on.

Know that thoughts are the constituents of the mind. Memories, desires, emotions, and habits are expressions of thoughts.

Thoughts have shapes, colors, weights, and their own life. They also have positive and negative endings. In the absence of such endings, the thought is neutral. Let's say that war is either good or bad. But if we remove good or bad, all that remains is war – it is neutral. Neutral here means the absence of judgment. Unfortunately, we are constantly flooded with positive and negative thoughts that keep our mind disturbed.

Thoughts also exhibit magnetism. This is because the basic energy of the creation is love, which is magnetic and dual (lover and loved). Thus, duality being the nature of creation, it is divided into the opposing polarities of attraction and repulsion. The mind also has both qualities. It attracts like-kinds of thoughts and repulses unlike thoughts.

The mind contains the four elements of creation: space, air, fire, and water. It does not have an earth element, which is why it is not visible to the naked eye. Space expands and contracts as needed. Similarly, the mind expands and contracts itself as a single point of concentration. The fluidity of expansion and contraction is what shows the illusionary nature of space. The illusionary nature of the mind is evident in that when we become aware of mind it disappears. Space is also necessary for creation to exist. Space allows the mind to exist, and we know its existence. Space also provides infinity to the mind. Time is perceived because of space; therefore, the more time you give to a thought, the more spacious it becomes (i.e., it expands and becomes more powerful). This is another important point and something you need to pay attention to.

The air element can be witnessed through the mind's invariable connection to our breathing. For example, If you hold your breath, your thoughts stop. Teachers of meditation place an emphasis on breathing technique in order to arrest the wandering mind. The connectivity, penetration and mobility of air coupled with the infinity of space allows our minds to connect to anywhere in the universe and attract any thoughts it wants. You can connect to thoughts from the mind of a NASA scientist in Texas, from a farm laborer in China, or from a nomad in Africa.

The fire element, due to its dual nature, contains the water element, its opposite. The former is evident from mind's ability to discriminate, as well as in its ability to rouse (or "fire up") emotions.

The water element can be seen in the mind's fluidity, the continual swirling of thoughts. When air does not touch water, it remains a flat, even surface. When we refuse the air, our mind becomes calm. Water also gives our mind a flexible shape. This flexibility, or fluidity, is a very important aspect of our understanding. The energy of our emotions and thoughts is meant to be fluid, so when it becomes stuck in any one part of the body, that part will get sick, much like stagnant water becomes a breeding ground for filth and decay because it is

20

not able to move. Take a moment to think on the enormity of this truth.

This subject may seem mind-boggling to some, even inconceivable, but that is what the mind is. The mind is a huge subject, so please bear with me. I will break it down into several parts so that it does not become overwhelming. Next, we will learn about the state of your mind, i.e., the conditioning of the mind.

Meanwhile, let us remain in peace,

Purandar

P.S. Read this again and again until you have thoroughly digested the nature of the mind.

3

COLORS

September 23, 2012

Dear Uma,

In this fall season, people travel to the Northeast to witness the changing colors of the leaves. The panorama of bright shades and warm hues creates a beautiful sight. This glorious landscape is a result of certain conditions: weather, the age of the leaves, etc. And just as the leaves respond to these conditions, so do you also respond to conditions: the conditions of your mind. You are what your mind is; physically, mentally, emotionally, and spiritually. The state of your being – what you are – is the result of the conditioning of many lifetimes, and these conditioning continue unabated until you stop them. First, let us examine the process.

Long before time immemorial, when creation did not exist, there was but a micro point of consciousness. Some call this "God." Having creative and expressive abilities within, there arose a sense of "I exist." Some phrase this as "I Am." This separateness created an element called "duality." To exist, space was needed, so space came into existence. The thought "I Am" created a vibration, and air came into being. The existence of space and air created a friction – the fire element. And again, with duality being the nature of creation, the element of water was created as an opposing element to fire.

Consciousness continued to express itself further. Due to its inherent magnetic properties, trillions of points of energy combined to take physical shapes; we call them planets. At this point, energy became dormant for a while. But the ability to "create and express" could not be stopped forever. And so, vegetation, animals, birds, and finally humans came into existence.

In humans, living consciousness expressed itself in the form of thought generation. The process continues still. Each thought – alive, energetic, and creative – multiplies itself in infinite directions, turning itself into a web of lighted threads. If you were to see it with your naked eye, it might look like an oval-shaped bird's nest surrounding your body.

If your belief is that you did not go through the evolutionary process, but simply came into being as human from the start, it is okay to hold onto this belief and move forward. However, the original thought – "I Am" – is still necessary for you to exist. This "I Am," being a separating thought, is what some call "ego." It is original, and a root thought of "mine and thine." As it moves forward, this thought continues the process of acquisition and disbursing of the thoughts of "mine" and "thine." This process of likes and dislikes by ego is represented by the present-day "you." Every tiny bit of our life is the result of likes and dislikes, of mine and thine. It is these likes and dislikes that give you the opposing polarities of joy and grief, happiness and pain, satisfaction and displeasure, contentment and worry, etc. This is known as the conditioning of the mind.

Many of us do not even recognize that our minds are conditioned, because it is a part of our everyday lives. Conditioning is defined as the sociological process of training individuals in a society to respond in a manner generally approved by the society in general and among peer groups within society. This conditioning is stronger than that of socialization, which refers to the process of inheriting norms, customs, and ideologies. Manifestations of social conditioning are vast. They are categorized as social patterns and structures, including, but not limited to, education, employment, entertainment, popular culture, religion, spirituality, and family life. The social structure in which an individual finds him or herself influences and can even determine their actions and responses within society.

The conditioning of the mind begins as soon as a child is born. Some conditioning of the mind is necessary for us to function as normal human beings. For example, a mother points to a chair and says to her baby, "Chair." After many repetitions, the child's mind accepts a certain shaped object as a chair. For day-to-day living, such conditioning is necessary. This conditioning continues until you die. The sources of the conditioning are not limited to society – they can result from religion teachings, the media, the Internet, personal conversations, and anything else that affects the mind. Notice how you see many advertisers repeating the same advertisements again and again; this is to condition your mind. Had DeBeers not advertised "Diamonds are forever," in the 1940s, we might view these hard, shiny stones differently today. Name brand clothing and accessories, and even celebrities are the product of this principle.

These conditions can be seen in certain impersonal assumptions we make. They include ideas like:

- Ours is the best basketball team in the NBA.
- Republicans, or Democrats, are hypocrites.
- My religion is superior to other religions.
- These articles are copycats.
- Asians are smart business persons.

- That airline has bad service.

To bring this concept down to a more personal level, conditioning has led us to embrace certain belief systems. Here are a few common (and conditioned) belief systems:

- I must have a house – a house in a decent location – a house in a decent location on a large lot – a large lot with a large house – a large house with all the amenities – a house with all the amenities that are better than those my friends or family members have.

- I must have a good job – a good job with an important title – an important title with a large paycheck – a large paycheck with a big bonus.

- My children must get a perfect high school grade average – my children must get a perfect high school grade average so they can graduate high school in the best standing – my children must graduate high school in the best standing so they can go to an Ivy League university.

- My reputation must be spotless – my reputation must be spotless so that it can remain intact – my reputation must remain intact because it is all I have.

Our personal likes and dislikes can also contribute to the conditioning of our mind. These likes and dislikes can often be traced back to our childhood. For example, your personal set of morals may cause you to expect certain behavior from others. When others fail to behave within your presupposed moral conditions, you may believe that they are immoral or bad.

Can you see how these conditioned morals can create conflicts? My purpose for this demonstration is to show that your mental conditioning has created bondage, limitations, or boundaries within which you behave and anticipate the reactions of others. Do you see how this conditioning can play a huge role in our daily lives? Take a few minutes to think about your own actions and reactions. Can you identify some of your personal conditioning? Why do you expect others to behave within your own limited guidelines when they ultimately cause you grief? This is an important point to remember in our larger discussion of achieving stress-free living.

These are your boundaries; these are your own expectations. And it is an inability to meet your own expectations or stay within your own boundaries that creates your frustrations and stress. Imagine, for a moment, that your mind is cleared of these boundaries. You will feel free, stress-free. Realize that your own mental conditioning (i.e. viewpoints, opinions, and belief systems) are the root cause of your worries and stress. You have created your own mental prison within which you are forcing yourself to stay. When you also understand that the words, thoughts, and actions of others are born from their own mental conditioning, you will have compassion toward them rather than anger, disgust, or frustration. The result will be improved relationships.

Conditioning creates a heavy web of thoughts around us; it prevent us from thinking outside the box. If you want to be free, you need to give up your viewpoints, concepts, belief systems, and, logically, any man-made moral systems. (When I say you must give up man-made moral systems, this does not translate into an allowance of criminal behavior; it does not mean you should seek to circumvent or break the laws of the land. Man-made views change according to time and place. Some laws are definitely never justified, so breaking these laws is not immoral.) What I want to convey is that your conscience is above man-made laws. Yet some man-made laws must be complied with so that life and society may function smoothly.

Notice one more thing: You own your mental conditioning. Your beliefs regarding your family, your job, your house, your morals – they are your own. And they are all manipulations of the ego. Remember: Ultimately, nothing is yours. So why not give up, rather than fighting to hold on to these things? What do you have to lose? Practically nothing.

A person once came to me and said, "I have daily fights with my wife. What should I do?" I replied, "Give up your viewpoints, opinions, and judgments." The man argued, "If I am right, why should I give up?" I further counseled, "Give up the need to be right. If you are right, then you are right; there is no need to prove it. Peace is more valuable than proving you are right – a need that arises from ego."

Finally, let us discuss the effect of time on conditioning of the mind. Know this: The conditioning of time is a most powerful cause of worries. (Like, what will happen tomorrow if that happens?....an eternal question in the moving caravan of thoughts!)

The human mind is conditioned by the division of time (i.e., past, present, and future). This three-dimensional timeframe is created by the movement of the earth on its axis and around the sun. Imagine for a moment what might happen if the earth stopped moving on its axis; the present could not become the past, nor is the future becoming the present. The present would simply remain the present. Think about this for a while. Try to hold the present moment in your awareness as long as you can. You will realize that time has not moved. It is the interception of light and shadow causes you to differentiate the time. Thus, our perception of time is an illusion.

There is no change in time. It is just an experience of light and darkness, which we calculate into days, months, and years. The earth needs space to move around. Yet our perception of that space is also an illusion. For example, let us say that you are going to your bank. You park your car, go into the bank, finish your banking, and came back to the parking lot an hour later. You are happy to see your car in the same spot. Now, scientists say that the earth moves at a speed of 1,040 miles an hour. Your car, placed on the earth, has also moved 1,040 miles in space though it is in the same earthly spot. And yet you do not see that difference. I am explaining these elements as you think of them in terms of past, present, and future – which are mental illusions! Can you realize that, in truth, the past does not exist except in your memories? Can you accept that the future exists only in your mind? You might be asking, "What does this have to do with my stress?" Do your worries not stem from thoughts of the future?

Now you observe your mind; it always moves to the past or the future but does not stay in the present. If your past is pleasant, your mind will enjoy the memories and conjure up future sweet scenes. If your past is full of miseries, your mind will create fears and worries. Now try to keep your mind in the present for a moment – not letting it wander to the past or the future. Though you may find this to be difficult, you will also find a momentous truth: <u>the mind does not exist.</u> The discovery that the mind does not exist in the present is important because of its implications. If the mind does not exist, how can you have stress? You have stress because you are always thinking of the past or the future.

We can all agree that the past is gone; it is history, a memory. There is nothing you can do about it, so why have regrets? We also know that the future is unpredictable, uncontrollable, and exists solely in the land of imagination (where mind likes to wander). Your worries and stress are the products of this land of imagination, this playground of the mind. And so we have come to the conclusion that your stress arises when you let your mind wander in the past or the future.

<u>Keep your mind in the present</u>. Stop thinking about the future, and worries won't come. Stop thinking about the past, and fears will not come. I know you will ask, "Why shouldn't I think of the future? If I don't, how can I plan for my life?" Wait; there is more to come.

Again, in your daily life activities, you need to obey the rules of past, present, and future. But for your inner purpose, don't let time rule your mind. Your internal world is your world only.

In presence, I remain,

Purandar

P.S. Know your conditioning and you will know the source of your fears and stress; it is that simple. Your conditioning stimulates different rates of vibration that create several zones, or layers, of the mind. These layers are connected, but can work independently to affect different parts of the body. Every thought affects each cell of the body.

Exercise

Try to be aware of the contents of your mind – how you habitually respond to persons and events. Study these interactions and begin to build a list of your own conditionings (likes, dislikes, viewpoints, etc.).

Notice how your reactions are due to your viewpoints and judgments. Now, compare your list of conditionings with the causes of your stress.

<u>My Notes</u>

4

ENERGY

January 1, 2013

Dear Uma,

On this New Year's Day, everybody seems so happy and relaxed. It makes me wonder what happened to all their worries. It is like a gigantic quantum leap has taken over humanity. Even early in the fall, weeks before Christmas, people begin to feel joyous and start looking forward to the happy days ahead. Such a massive change in the energy of thinking patterns is felt by everybody. The same is true for negative energies, such as the massive destructive energy of war that created the blasts of Hiroshima and Nagasaki. These two opposite examples of positive and negative are microscopic examples of the totality of energy. Now realize, both these massive shifts were forms of thought before they entered into our collective perception. Scriptures say that the entirety of creation was once in a thought form.

Physics cannot describe energy properly, as it is infinite in nature and attributes. Everything is one or another form of energy; your house, furniture, fixtures, and other possessions are all coalesced forms of energy. Our body is a form of aggregated points of energy. Even our emotions and thoughts are subtle forms of energy. Different people have different bodies, different thoughts, and different emotions. This is because different people carry different sets of energy.

Energy cannot be destroyed. It can, however, be transmuted, transferred, or released. Energy can display a rainbow of colors, or simply be transparent. It can also assume any shape. Energy emits movement. These movements carry all the properties of their energy source, causing an attachment between like kinds of energy; ultimately, that energy is transferred to the subject of the attachments.

Everything is energy. The energy that makes up "you" – just like the energy that makes up the members of your family, your friends, and even your home, neighborhood, and society at large – has the ability to influence not just your own emotions, thoughts, actions, and reactions, but also the emotions, thoughts, actions, and reactions of others. The purpose of this illustration is to emphasize the point that energies affect and influence each other. Your thoughts and emotions – such as joy or grief, excitement or depression, feelings of failure or success – affect everything, from the outcome of a situation to other members of your family.

Science tells us that energy comes in different currents: positive, negative, and neutral. The neutral current, in terms of the mind, is equanimity. Equanimity is complete peace with no movement toward either the negative or the positive side. Sages advise us to maintain this equanimity. You will soon come to experience that the virtues of equanimity are far more valuable than you ever realized.

Whatever you think, speak, or do is energy. When the present becomes the past, your thoughts, words, and actions become memories of an event. Memory is a form of thought; consequently, it is also a form of energy and you carry this energy – your memories – with you. The retention ability of our consciousness is the foundation of the law of Karma. When you are freed from your physical body upon death, these memories survive and cause another body's formation. Remember, no form comes into being without having first been a thought. Some call this the cycle of birth and death.

When you consider that you have the retained the memories of many lifetimes, it is nothing but a bottomless pit of thoughts. In fact, the retention ability of the mind is so pervasive that I myself have seen half sentences, even words, countless web pages, fast moving scenes from a video game, a broken song, a small insignificant event in a distant past all survived in my memory bank. Anything that happened to our body's atoms also survives in the memory bank.

Most of us have no ability to recall a past life's memories at will, but that does not mean that they are lost. In fact, if you can remain in a thoughtless condition for a sufficient amount of time, you will remember a past life's events. This is important to understand, as our present life is conditioned by these memories. By extending this idea of Karmic energy, we can see how the individual Karma of your family members can unite and produce energy fields that affect all of you. Similarly, the Karma of nations affects the entire citizenry of the country. It is very mysterious and scary, too, when we cannot seem to identify the cause of the effect through the use of conventional wisdom. Your own bottomless pit of memories can cause you stress, worry, and unhappiness if you do not know how to handle them. Just know that you are covered with a cloud of energies that may or may not be beneficial to your wellbeing.

One of the most important things you can do is to think positive thoughts, speak kind words, and do good deeds. The importance of positive thoughts, words, and deeds cannot be overestimated, as their energy is added to that which already surrounds you. All you can do is to produce good energy and to surround yourself with sources of love, joy, and peace. The vibrations of these positive energies will produce a covering cloud around you, protecting you. And, since your energy will affect others, the members of your family will also feel peace and happiness. Know that these are not empty words or abstract ideas. It does have substantial affects on you and your surroundings.

To do this:

- Be aware of your thoughts at all times.
- Resolve to entertain only good thoughts.
- Speak only soothing words.
- Act lovingly and compassionately.

Regard your thoughts, words, and actions as invisible garments that you wear all the time.

Energy is very subtle – so much so that most of us are not aware of it. How, then, do you protect yourself from the energy of other people and the energy of your surroundings? You need to be aware of it, from moment-to-moment. Begin by practicing self-awareness. How do you feel? Are you peaceful or agitated? Are you worried or joyful? Are you tense? The moment you identify the emotions you are experiencing, step aside, as if you are an outside observer of your body. Watch the emotions without being judgmental or involved. The trick is to simply be aware of your emotions, but – at the same time – not to think about them. Watch your emotions as long as you can or until they disappear from your awareness. What you are doing is rejecting the negative patterns that surround you. <u>This is the truth: In awareness, the mind does not survive and, without the help of the mind, emotions do not survive.</u> Emotions and thoughts are intertwined; they affect each other.

Once you recognize your own state of being, any change to that state should alert you. When you are meeting someone or going somewhere, check the state of your emotions and thoughts before you start. Check your emotions and thoughts again when you leave that person or place. If you feel differently than you did to begin with, you have been affected by the energy of the person or place you visited. You can use the light property of energy to protect yourself from unwanted energies. The different colors of light produce different forms of energy – both positive and negative. There are three basic colors: blue, red, and yellow. All other colors are a combination of these three. Each color carries its own unique energy, which can be witnessed in our responses to them. For example, when you see blue sky or blue waters, you feel peace and calm, and you may feel the urge to rest. Red is more invigorating and is also associated with activity as well as anger. On the positive side, yellow governs happiness, creativity, and optimism, while it represents betrayal, ego, and cowardice on the negative side. White is the color of purity, protection, and transparency. If you are going to meet someone or enter a place that you do not like or is making you apprehensive, cover yourself with white, transparent silver, gold, or deep blue colors of light.

Fortunately, energy is alive, intelligent, and conscious. Therefore, it is possible to remove it or invite it in with a mental command. All you have to do to remove an unwanted energy is to concentrate on it and ask it firmly to leave. Likewise, you can invite other energy to come into your being. An example of this would be prayer. Every prophet and every religion has advised prayer. If you believe in God or All That Is, you can call upon its help, energy, and protection. Prayers protect those who believe in the power of prayer and invoke them. Such things will not work without faith in the Almighty, in yourself, and in your intentions to invoke help.

Observe your body now to discover which parts may not be feeling well. Usually, you will find that pain resides in your heart – especially if the ego is involved – but also look for pain in other areas. If you find discomfort, you are already affected by an unwanted energy. Concentrate on the discernible location of the ailment and firmly ask the energy to leave. (Be advised that the unwanted energy may affect different parts of the body, and you may not even recognize it.) Once, I was affected by a persistent cough that would not go away with any medicine. Finally, when I removed the energy through pointed concentration and command, I was instantly healed.

Faith requires an unwavering belief in the Almighty and in yourself. Do not confuse faith with blind belief. Faith is an inner conviction, a knowingness of something as matter of fact. It requires no force. On the other hand, blind belief comes from the mind and requires force, argument, and conflict. When everything goes awry, faith in what you believe will keep you going. And, when your faith is tested, if you succeed in passing that test, the enormous energy generated by the sheer force of your intent can and will change your circumstances in your favor.

A widely accepted spiritual belief is the idea that the universe is always working perfectly, as a whole and in parts, for you personally. If you are in an imperfect condition, the entire universe will be in an imperfect condition (since an imperfect part cannot be part of a perfect condition). This cannot happen, as a perfect God cannot make an imperfect universe. Whatever your circumstances are, they must be perfect in the totality of the universe. Otherwise, the universe cannot work perfectly.

We judge persons or events as good or bad, acceptable or unacceptable, or in terms of likes or dislikes. Our judgments are limited by our own limited knowledge of the events, persons, or anticipated future impacts. This makes these judgments imperfect. Since you do not know the future, it is very difficult for you to accept adverse conditions as perfect for you. This will be the stress test of your faith. Acceptance of present events, circumstances, or persons in your life to be "as it is" or "as perfect as it can be" is made easier when you accept the fact that your judgment is limited by your own limited knowledge. Your knowledge is not perfect because you cannot know how future events will turn out. It's time to acknowledge that you have no choice but to accept this and move on to take the next appropriate step.

In short, when you do not like something:

- Know that your judgment is not perfect.
- Know that you cannot know the future effects of what you do not like.
- Know that there is a lesson for you to learn.
- Know that everything happens for a reason that you do not know.
- Know that everything happens in its own time.
- Know that time changes everything.

Last but not least, the mind – being consciousness expressed – has an unlimited ability to create. All forms before your eyes were thoughts prior to their worldly existence. In the same way, all emotions are thoughts made manifest. You can create happiness and health. You can also create sorrow, pain, or stress. It is your choice. This concept applies to all persons, from the members of your household to the individuals at your place of employment. Since everyone is creating, there is a mutual creation, moving, static, or destructive, depending upon the strength and intensity of the creator. Now, look at your own circumstances as your own creation. If you do not like it as it is, you can reverse the process. Go back and review your own mindset, patiently, as a long gone past. You will find yourself to be your own creator.

Create empty space in your being, and you will create peace. With peace, beneficial energies will flow in your life.

In peace, with you,

Purandar

Points to Remember

- Realize the infinite power and expression of energy.
- All energies can be transmuted into other forms.
- All imperfections and adversities are limited judgments.
- Energy can respond to your mental command.

Exercise

Watch your emotions four times a day. If you find yourself to be stressed or worried, take a step back from yourself. Observe your stress and worries as an objective outsider, without being judgmental. Write down your observations in the "My Notes" section. Make sure to record the date. One month later, come back and review what you wrote.

My Notes

5

THE WAVES IN THE OCEAN

March 14, 2014

Dear Uma,

A dog is barking outside and I wonder what kind of emotions it is feeling. Is it feeling fear? I see a rare Amazonian bird on a television program, dancing to attract a mate. Where does this emotion come from? Intelligence? Heart? Or just plain instinct? Everything, sentient or insentient, is affected by emotions. It could be the calm waters of the ocean, a roaring tsunami, cool breezes, a ferocious blizzard, a summer storm with cracks of lightning, or a devastating forest fire. All are apt descriptions of emotions. There is much more to learn about emotions than the average human being could imagine. Emotions produce stress or happiness.

We all have emotions of various kinds. This is because our thoughts generate emotions. Remember that energy can be positive, negative, or neutral, and all emotions are forms of energy. Love, joy, and peace are examples of positive emotions. Hatred, envy, and sadness are examples of negative emotions. Ego colors your emotions with "mine" and "thine" separations. Your mental conditioning causes your reactions. In turn, the energy that is released by your thoughts turns into a positive or negative emotion.

Whether you create positive or negative emotions depends on your reactions. For instance, if there is an event affecting two people, one might call the experience positive, and the other might deem it negative. Each individual will respond to events and circumstances within the limitations of his or her mental conditioning. It is your mental structuring that defines your interpretations and causes your reactions. That is why your reactions are actually more important than the event itself. If you lose your job, your employer might consider the event as simply a way to save on payroll expenses. You, however, will view it as a loss of income. Your children might worry about their pocket money. Your spouse might plan to cut back on spending. Or you may take it as an opportunity to strike out on your own. What occurs is one single event, but it is experienced through many different perceptions.

While your negative emotions may feel like a natural part of life, they become a problem when you give them too much time. Emotions, being energy, must be flowing and moving. But when you fixate on negative emotions, that energy tends to clump together. When emotions aggregate, they become stagnant, glued down to one place. Often, when an area of the body is experiencing discomfort or disease, it is the same place where energy has become stuck. For instance, a lack of love resulting in loneliness may affect the heart or the pancreas. Too much stress may affect your heart or your brain. Too much rushing in your daily life may affect your knees.

It is not just your emotions that you must be aware of when you react to situations. You may need to unlearn your reactions in order to remain still in the face of another person's energy. Let's say that somebody is angry at you. Most individuals will respond in kind. But that anger is the problem of the angry person, not yours. Because of the reflective nature of creation, the energy from the other person's anger is projected onto you, so you instinctively fight back. Yet when you become aware that the anger you are feeling is the other person's problem, not yours, that anger will not affect you. You will naturally remain quiet. Similarly, other negative energies or ego issues such as envy or unhappiness may not be your problem. They are always the problem of the person who carries them. When you react to the other person's negative energy, it manifests itself as similar energy within you.

Most of us have pain buried deep within the recesses of our subconscious. Our equal reaction to negative energy brings forth this pain to the surface and accentuates it, causing even more suffering.

Emotions are motions of energy in action. They are the children of thoughts. They cannot survive without thoughts. They travel down memory lane on the wings of hope and expectations or of failure, disappointments, and hurts.

Some emotions are derived from your past. Here I mean not just the past of this life, but of many lives before your present body. You may say, "I don't have any memory of such past events, so how can these affect me?" My dear, it will affect you. Find an emotion or a behavior pattern that you act upon automatically. It may have a root in your past. For example, are you afraid of fire, water, or heights? You may have previously died of such causes. Are you overreacting to certain thoughts, behaviors, emotions, or situations? You may have experiences buried in the past that are so strong the effects are still being felt.

> Let me open up. In this life, if somebody praises me or appreciates me, tears will well up and roll down my cheeks. The root cause of this is not an event from my

current life, but from one of my previous bodies. In the past, I lived the life of a female slave. I was abused by everybody and did not receive an iota of respect. My need for appreciation was so emotionally ingrained in my being that now, when someone appreciates or praises me, tears will flow. In yet another body, I was a well-respected and sought-after public speaker. During a public speech, I took a very unpopular position. People did not like this and responded by throwing shoes and other items at me. I was deeply humiliated. It left a deep scar in my soul. In this life, whenever I try to speak publically, I automatically choke, and my eyes begin to well up. Both of these scars, stemming from experiences in previous lives, were removed only when I became aware of the incidents. Many choose not to believe this, but that is their problem and not my concern.

Obviously, emotions are also generated by present memories associated with infinite subjects. In the case of a foreclosure, you might think about how hard it was to find, negotiate, and acquire your property. You might lament your children's memories, and all the precious times you shared with your spouse here. You relive your memories at the same time you are dwelling on thoughts of losing the house, which puts you in an emotional zone. This creates a multitude of fears; fear of homelessness, fear of family turmoil, fear of a tarnished reputation, etc. As a result, negative emotions such as self-pity and regret arise.

Do you blame yourself for making wrong decisions in the past? Remember two things: (1) Everybody makes mistakes, and (2) to make a decision in the present and to make a judgment in hindsight are two very different things. It is easy to criticize a decision when you are under a new set of circumstances. Changed circumstances, changed thinking patterns, changed surroundings, etc., allow you to evaluate your decision from a new perspective. It doesn't bode well for you to judge past decisions based on your current circumstances.

This is a recipe for self-pity, which leads to depression and robs you of your natural abilities to think and act. It throws you into an ocean of confusion that prevents you from dealing effectively with the situation at hand. It makes you lazy, angry with yourself, and angry with others. To hide your depression, you can start blaming others and the external systems we live within. This train of thought also affects your work performance and your closest relationships. It can create a wall between you and your colleagues, family, and friends. It is a strange irony that, at this time, when you need a stable mind the most, you lose that stability.

When you find yourself falling into the clutches of depression, recognize the situation immediately. Do not give time to depressing thoughts of self-pity. Be aware of your mental condition at all times.

Feeling guilty for not making the right decision is like punishing an innocent person. There are many hidden causes behind an event to happen. Your past is only a small part of these occurrences. The first step to freeing yourself from self-pity is to be aware of your condition. Self-pity or self-criticism robs you of your ability to change your circumstances. However, If you harbor no regrets, you will find you no longer have cause for stress.

It is also very important that you remember that you and your actions are only a small part of any situation or event. There are an infinite number of factors that came together to cause the situation. You played but a small part in causing the outcome, so blaming yourself for the whole thing that was largely out of your control, is erroneous thinking.

Similarly, blaming your troubles on the faults you find in others does nothing but cause you even more pain. Everybody lives within the circle of their mind. When you are focused on finding a scapegoat, your mind is consumed with thoughts of blame. "Why did so-and-so do this?" "Why didn't he explain?" "Why did she make this mistake?" These don't help you at all. Even as you should not blame yourself, so should you refrain from blaming others. If you would not treat *yourself* like this, then neither is it right to treat others this way.

So what can you do about these emotions? Think of a few reliable friends whose wisdom you can trust. Talk about your emotions openly with them. Bringing your emotions out into the open will help draw them into conscious awareness. In the bright light of day, they will, ultimately fade away and disintegrate. What you are doing is disbursing the energy and moving it away from you. If you do not feel comfortable discussing this with friends, you can write your unwanted emotions down on a piece of paper and burn it. This is a simple rule: When a mass of energy is contained in a small place, it becomes concentrated and more solid. By bringing your emotions (which are energy) out into the open, their power is weakened. Openness is a virtue. <u>Being open makes you free.</u>

Everyone encounters times when they feel confused and in turmoil, not knowing what to do. This confusion arises from the contradictions between two opposite forces of emotion. One force tells you to fight back against your present situation; the other tells you to let it go. Confusion arises because the first force has not been relinquished while, at the same time, the second force has not been embraced.

You must allow the situation to evolve. Fighting, resisting, or even delaying this evolution requires you to expend unnecessary energy, which causes a drain both physically and mentally. Many times, patience is the only solution to the confusion. Surrender to your higher power; it will help.

How many times in the past have you experienced the truth that there are always at least two or more sides to every story? Know that all events have two sides. If you are in a situation where you are fearful of losing something, your fear is born of your attachment. Yet, if you see the situation as an opportunity and a freedom, then you are practicing detachment and will be able to more easily move on. Detachment from the property, event, or relationship gives you the freedom and opportunity to move to a different location, make new friends, etc. If you change your perspective toward the property, event or relations, you will be able to see the whole picture and release unwanted energies.

The decision to label a situation as good or bad depends upon your perspective, which is often shaped by past experiences stored in your mind. Do not confuse this with reality. In truth, there is no right or wrong way, nothing bad nor good. Take a moment to ponder this. What you consider bad today may turn out to be good tomorrow, or vice versa.

How do you know for sure what the future holds? Do you know for certain that your home is going to be foreclosed on? Is it a fact, or is it only fear that you are going to lose your job? Can you be certain of the day you will die?

Who knows? You might win the lottery today. Perhaps your home will burn down before foreclosure. You may even land a better job, one that you have never even considered. Anything can happen. Your best-laid plans may count for nothing.

Likewise, you may find that help materializes from where you least expect it. Remember that the future you are imagining is based upon past experiences. Your past experiences, being limited, are limiting to your viewpoint as well. What is the use of worrying about the future when you do not – cannot – know it?

Remember what we said earlier: Do not indulge in these thoughts! Know that unnecessary and frequent thinking on the same negative subject acts as a disease. Stay away from it.

In peace, with you,

Purandar

PS: Remove all emotional aspects from any expected event, outcome, person, relationship and you will be free from the stress. This is million-dollar advice.

Points to Remember

- Worries are thoughts mixed with emotions.
- Worries are fears of the future, which are not real.
- Worries are made up of energy that can be disbursed.
- The future is impossible to know.
- Changing your perspective will allow you to see reality differently.
- Think of the positive aspects of seemingly negative events, such as a foreclosure, getting fired, or some such other event; learn to view it as an opportunity to make necessary changes.
- Awareness is the first step in the removal of emotions.

Exercise

Begin by finding a quiet and comfortable place where you can sit. Take deep breaths – inhaling, holding the breath, and exhaling in an equal amount of time. (For example, inhale for four beats, hold in the breath for four beats, and exhale for four beats.) Continue to focus on your breathing until your thoughts die down.

Bring your awareness to your heart center; concentrate on an imaginary point of blue or white light in that spot. Begin to enlarge the light internally until it fills your entire body. Continue to let the light spread out externally, covering your outer body and moving outward as far as you can imagine.

Bring your emotion into your awareness, and surrender them to the light. Let the light dissolve them. Keep the light in your awareness, moving back and forth until the thoughts and emotions dissolve. Remain in awareness of the light for a minute or so afterwards, then you are free to shift your attention elsewhere.

You may need to practice his exercise few times until your emotions lose their grip on you.

<u>My Notes</u>

6

IT'S ALL ABOUT ME

April 18, 2013

Dear Uma,

Eons ago "I Am" arose from nothingness and creation was brought into being. You, I, this, and that became reflective expressions of the original "I Am."

In this intricate creation, there are both subtle and obvious elements. What we can perceive with our five senses (what we can see, hear, taste, smell or touch) are obvious elements. It is what we *cannot* perceive that are known as subtle elements. The more subtle the element, the more powerful the force. The intelligence of the mind is full of subtle elements. Yet even more subtle than mind-intelligence is the ego. Mind and intelligence are instruments of the ego.

The ego's definite identification is separateness – "mine and thine." The ego is considered reflective – it is a phantom reflection of the soul. Since it is subtle, it is harder to perceive. However, its influence is felt all over. If I were to state that all of your stress, worries, and fears are the projections of ego, it would not be wrong. We have spent considerable time analyzing the mind because the ego works through the mind. Your ego works through your mind since the mind is less subtle than the ego. Therefore, if you develop a habit of tracing your ego's presence in everything, then working with the mind will be a lot easier.

To make the presence of the ego obvious, let us cite some examples:

- You have a fear of losing your home. Underneath this is a fear of losing your reputation among friends and relatives, because your ego perceives this as, "I am not less than others." Also, underneath this is a fear of being homeless, because your ego says, "I am better than those homeless people."

- You are afraid of losing your job. Underneath this is a fear of not being able to provide for yourself and your family (pay your bills, put food on the table, etc.), because your ego says, "I am capable of doing anything. This hurts my pride. I am not a beggar."

- You have a fear of illness or death. Underneath this is the ego's belief that, "I am healthy and indestructible; I can fight death and can survive."

- You are worried about losing a promotion at work. Underneath this is a fear of losing control over a situation because your ego says, "I am a better manager. Nobody can do a better job than me. Without my management, the project will collapse."

Other examples of ego manifestations are:

- You want the best-perceived seat at the event.

- You treat your gardener and your professor differently.

- You believe your home is the best looking one in the neighborhood.

- You must win this game, promotion, award, etc.

- You must reach the meeting on time.

Did you notice the commonality of separateness in all of these statements? Can you sense the contrast between "mine and thine" that lies behind these assertions?

The list can go on and on, as ego is a normal reflection of ourselves in the world. So, what is the problem with ego? There are, in fact, several problems:

- Ego creates fears and worries.

- Ego creates false pride.

- Ego creates relationship issues.

- Ego wants everything, irrespective of desirability or need.
- Ego creates grief upon the failure to fulfill one's expectation.
- Ego creates anger, conflict, and unhappiness.
- Ego creates envy among close friends.
- Ego creates stress in anticipation.
- Ego breeds desire – the root of many evils.
- Ego is the cause of hurt and pain.

This list is not complete; it can be extended to every area – even the smallest area of life.

Ego also affects groups and nations. Look at these statements:

- Ours is the most powerful nation on earth.
- My religion is better than yours.
- Ours is the largest economy in the world.
- We Americans can do better than others.

Mankind has battled for centuries to destroy the ego, but it is still part of our existence. Spiritualists will tell you that the ego will even survive death. The ego cannot be completely destroyed, even in a case of near-perfect self-realization. Masters of spiritual wisdom have differed when asked to identify the end point of the ego. Should universal dissolution come to pass, the consciousness of ego will be destroyed; it would become as a "point" of pure awareness. (The word "point" is used here just for explanatory purposes in the absence of a better word.)

What is ego? The ego is commonly known as "I-ness." Children of the ego exhibit such things as separateness, resentment, or resistance to resolving their problems. Jealousy, greed, immaturity, refusal to accept responsibility, and blame games are all issues of the ego. In addition, all personalized identifications are related to the ego. The ego functions via judgments of superiority and inferiority, good and bad, worthy and unworthy.

Why does the ego matter? The ego will cloud your objectivity. It will get in the way of accepting a solution. It will produce an attachment to possessions, relationships, or whatever you value. It will make it harder to let go.

Any thought that starts with "My" is a manifestation of the ego. "My house," "My property," "My savings," "My memories", all are red flags that indicate you are cooperating with the ego rather than seeking unbiased solutions to your problems. The ego will spawn false emotions, assumptions, and illusions of reality to prevent you from accepting a valid solution. Your logic, judgments, and viewpoints can be twisted to suit the ego's designs.

The nature of the world being reflective, the easiest way to identify the ego's play in your life is when you observe the ego in others. That ego, in turn, is a reflection of your own ego. This may sound strange, but it is nature's way of teaching us. If you find someone obstinate in making concessions, stop and check to see if you are stuck in *your* opinions, too.

If you find someone who seems to be demanding too much, stop and check to see if you, too, are exhibiting high expectations. If you find something to be unacceptable, stop and check to see if it mirrors your own reality. This is tough advice, but I am on your side, so I must state it like it is. In these letters, I intend to provide you the keys to peace in your current turmoil.

If you are at war with someone, the ego will be the commander in chief of your army. Why do I say it like that? Your primary statement when addressing the issue will begin with "I" or "My." That "I" is your ego talking. Do you want to find the solution to your stress? Then your attention must be on the issue of stress, not on "I."

Remember that the ego is very subtle. It can throw off a good solution with subtle emotions. For example, I have often seen a property lost to foreclosure just because ego was playing its tricks until the last minute. If you are stuck holding a certain position in the negotiation process, a subtle ego might be in play.

Feelings of superiority or inferiority, engaging in power-play games, obstinacy, pride, trying to save face in front of relatives and friends, and refusal to recognize the realities of a situation (such as an approaching deadline) are all prime examples of the ego at work. The ego can be your worst enemy.

So, how do you keep the ego out? It is not easy, but you must do it. In the hierarchy of awareness, the ego is a phantom awareness of "Being-ness." In the hierarchy of subtlety and power, the ego lies above the objective mind, intelligence, and bodily perceptions, but below your true Self. In common terminology, the mind, intelligence, and body can serve the ego, but ego vanishes in the presence of your true Self.

Since time immemorial, spiritual masters have suggested various ways of removing or controlling the ego. But humanity is still struggling with ego and will continue to do so, since it is impossible for most people to exist without it. However, it *is* possible to get relief from ego-created problems, regardless of your level of spiritual evolution. The mind and intelligence are both vehicles of the ego; through them the ego directs you. You have the choice of working through your mind or getting help from your true divine Self, which is the boss of the ego. In the case of the former, you are unlikely to succeed in controlling the ego, since the mind is below the ego in the hierarchy of awareness. But your true Self, which is above the ego, is the boss – it can get the job done.

Separateness (i.e., you and I are different; "mine and thine") is both the basic trait of the ego and the source of its power.

Your attachment to your reputation, house, children, etc. is all rooted in the expression of the ego. There are also group egos, as well as national egos. Examine your thoughts and you will invariably see this truth.

The ego likes to control. It seeks to control situations, relationships, persons, events, minuscule details – everything. If you find yourself controlling, or even wanting to control any of these elements in your own life, know that your ego has taken control of yourself. You have become a slave of your ego. However, if you do just the opposite of controlling, your ego is diminished. To give up control is to surrender.

As stated earlier, the ego is a reflection of the soul. In the realization of this truth, the illusory nature of the ego will be revealed. In the light of this consciousness, just for that moment, the ego does not exist. In simple terms, if you make a practice of being aware of your ego, even momentarily, your ego will have no effect in those moments. Each awareness will reduce the size of your ego, rendering your diminished ego less capable of harm.

Another way to do this is to view your issues as separate from you. Envision yourself handling the issues as an advisor or a trustee, someone who has no personal interest in the outcome. If you mentally separate yourself from the issues, you will reap several benefits. You will assess and evaluate each action objectively and, therefore, without stress. You will find that your relations with others will improve. Your blood pressure will go down substantially as you will not be thinking of saving face. When you give up your ego, you will no longer be overly concerned about the opinions of others; you will truly be a free person.

You will also find that giving up the ego will reduce your anger, adjust your expectations, and remove any ideas of superiority. If you are easily offended at the slightest change in someone's voice, your ego is at work. In such cases, I suggest you observe your feelings, the sensations in your body, and the nature of the energy. In just a few minutes, you will find that the energy will dissolve. After a few such practice sessions, nobody will be able to hurt or insult you.

Your ego may also appear when you are complaining about others, their work, their comments, etc. Pay careful attention to how you think, speak, and act. This will make you increasingly aware of your ego's ploys. Once you become aware of your ego, it loses its power.

You are now passing through a critical period of learning life's lessons. Many people hardly ever think of the ego and its destructive abilities. They assume that theirs is normal behavior. Macho images, aggressive behavior, and putting others down are self-damaging attitudes that does more damage to yourself than others. In a time when you need to make critical decisions, you need to get rid of these elements.

In the end, when the ego vanishes into a "point" of pure awareness – an awareness that is omnipresent, omnipotent, and omniscient – love and peace remain.

In peace, I find solutions,

Purandar

PS: Once I made a list of ten persons against whom I felt superior in knowledge, experience, by birth or for some other reason. This turned into a huge moment of self-discovery for me. As I expanded my list, I realized that, unknowingly, I had been separating myself from others. I followed this up by making a list of the individuals around whom I felt inferior. Ego was doing its job in both instances.

Points to Remember

When you are alone, peaceful, and rested attempt to be aware of your thoughts, but do not think.

- Self-observation is an invaluable skill to develop.
- Be aware of your emotions, and watch how your body reacts to them.
- Know what and whom you tend to criticize; this is your self-projection
- Identify what angers you most; take note of the frequency and intensity of your outbursts.
- Be defenseless. Be exposed. You will not have to defend, protect, preserve or hide anything. You will gain immense strength, freedom and be stress-free.

Exercise

Compose yourself in a meditative state, as usual. Clear your thoughts. Bring your consciousness inside your body. See or imagine your body in a bubble of white or golden light.

While staying inside the bubble, expand your consciousness in every direction, all around you. Your bubble should begin expanding. Imagine that your bubble covers the entire universe. Feel the energy inside the bubble. See the light surrounding your body, extending in every direction. You are infinite. Stay like this for a minute or so.

Start making your bubble smaller and smaller, very slowly. Make sure to maintain your sense of the energy and light. It comes closer and closer to your body. Now, you will be shrinking your body's perception as well. As you continue squeezing your body's consciousness, it will become more and more difficult.

Make your heart center the main point of your focus. Continue retracting your consciousness, bringing it closer and closer to your heart center as it becomes smaller. Press on until your consciousness is so small that it is barely perceptible – no more than a single point. Now, you have returned to your beginning. Remain focused on this point for as long as you can (anywhere from a few seconds to few minutes).

End your meditation and slowly become aware of your surroundings. What you have done is compacted your universal and bodily consciousness into powerful, atomic energy, capable of destroying the world, but still silent.

My Notes

7

BOOMERANG

April 27 2013

Dear Uma,

You may be asking, "What is the role of Karma here?" Consider that Karma is an event that causes you stress or joy. As we have discussed, an event may occur due to multiple causes. One cause may be obvious to you, but what is not obvious is the operation of the Law of Karma. The Law of Karma states that for every action there is an equal reaction. Since everything is essentially energy, whatever you think, speak, or do produces energy. That act, which produces energy, will also produce an equal amount of compensatory energy. This means that whatever you do, there will be a result.

This simplicity of the Law of Karma stops here. I would venture to say that a substantial majority of persons, including believers in Karmic principles, do not comprehend the true functioning of Karmic Law.

The first principle addresses memory. Remember that whatever you do becomes a thread of memory. That memory is a thought. All the rules of thoughts now apply to it. As we learned earlier, thoughts have a magnetic property. They will attract like-kinds of energy. Thoughts, being energy, cannot be destroyed. Thus, these memories remain with you and become part of you (i.e., your mind). Also, remember that the mind survives physical death. This means that you may not receive the fruits of your actions in this lifetime, but in the next or even further down the road. What you must understand is that your actions – your memories – are energy that has become a part of your "Being."

The next Karmic principal concerns the idea of "group Karma." Because of the interconnectedness of creation, there is no Karma that is purely individual. Let's work through an example to help you understand the concept of group Karma. Let's say that you are involved in an accidental auto collision as a result of your previous Karma. Now, let's look at how many people are connected by this accident. The other party involved in the collision will be affected by the event. The owner of the auto body shop where you take your car to be repaired will be affected by the event. Even the mechanic who ends up working on your car is affected. Now, consider this: A main Karmic cause of this accident is that you owed a debt to the auto body shop owner in a previous life. By paying to have your car fixed at his shop, you are fulfilling your debt to him.

But the causes go even deeper. This event also happened because the auto body owner needed to pay the employee who worked on your car (which may be a present-life Karma for the auto body owner!). And, to take the theory a step further, what if that employee needed money to pay his utility bill for the month? Perhaps the employee also had a debt to the owners of the utility company in a previous life, or maybe the utility company needed to collect payments for this month's bills in order to pay its suppliers. This chain continues until the entirety of the group Karma is realized.

You could easily see this principal illustrated if we could to draw a diagram connecting the dots of actions and reactions across the entire earth. The intricate web would continue to spread until it connected all of humanity. This is the interconnectedness – the oneness – of the universe. It is this concept that accounts for the timing of your Karmic rewards; the timing requires the synchronicity and the coordination of all people's Karma, in order to deliver fair treatment.

Did you notice how the consequences of the main event – the car crash – took place at a later time? Even if the accident happened today, the full consequences of this Karmic event may not occur immediately, or even over the next few weeks.

And the main event itself – the accident – could actually be a Karmic result of actions taken in the previous lives of any of the persons involved. Thus, we see the interconnectedness, but also note that the time and space across which these connections occur may be different. It is a cosmic domino effect that takes place across various dimensions of reality.

If you're feeling lost at this point, or helpless to escape the intricacies of Karma, don't worry – you're not alone. As I said before, even devout believers of Karmic Law may fail to grasp the full magnitude of its workings in their lives. Just keep the principles of memory and interconnectedness in the back of your mind as we continue with the next topic.

Have you ever heard the saying, "You reap what you sow?" This idea leads to the logical conclusion that you eventually have to face up to the consequences of your actions. Whatever you experience – whether a thought, word, or event – is the harvest of your previous Karma. We can also conclude that the experienced effect had an initial cause and that this effect will become a new cause. It is this idea that leads us to draw the logical conclusion that whatever you are experiencing now – whether a thought, word, or event – is the harvest of previous Karma. It seems to be a vicious cycle and one that is difficult to break. But don't despair.

When you think, speak, or act, a motion of the energy is created. Energy has magnetic properties that cause it to attach to the creator. When performing Karma, generally you have a thought that you are doing it. When I am writing this, a thought passes through my mind that I am writing or this writing is mine. This makes me the owner and doer of the deed. Memories of work being done and done by me are combined and attached to my mental body. A third thought is that I expect the results of my action to benefit myself. Now all three thoughts, as energy, will attach to each other and form a binding bond around me. Still there is more.

There are five required elements to make the effects of Karma possible:

1. Time
2. Place
3. Instruments
4. Results
5. Knower

In order for Karma to be delivered, the timing must be right for all parties involved. In addition, there must be a place where the effects of Karma can be realized for each participant. All the appropriate instruments (i.e., humans, objects, animals, energies, etc.) must be ready for the execution of the Karmic event. The Karmic event will produce a domino effect, which will lead to various results for everyone involved (including their reactions, which will cause another cycle of events). Finally, this equation must have an executor – a Knower.

It is necessary for there to be one who knows the Karma of all humans. The Knower must be capable of discerning exactly what will happen in each case. Who can be such a capable entity? Who knows the past Karmas of all involved, and also knows the resultant effects in each case, with a precise coordination of place and timing? Some people call this entity "God." All these elements must be in play for Karma to be realized.

So, why does there seem to be a delay between the execution of your thoughts, words, and deeds and the point at which you receive the fruits of your labor? The coordination of time and place for the entire group involved in the event is necessary so that all parties involved will receive their due effects. Because this is not always immediately possible, there is a delay. And it is this delay that causes reincarnation.

Some religions do not believe in reincarnation, but that is their concern. My job is to explain reincarnation logically so that we can understand its role in the Law of Karma. Since the body is destructible, there must be something indestructible that will suffer or enjoy the fruits that are due them at the time when all the necessary elements can be properly structured. This indestructible aspect of your being is the energy of your Karma that becomes part of your mind. Your mind, in turn, becomes part of the shell that carries your soul to next body. This brings us to reincarnation.

How do you keep yourself stress-free and live a normal, happy life under the Law of Karma? To help you achieve these objectives, there are certain mental virtues that need to be cultivated. Whether you believe in God or not, whether you are a spiritual person or not, is immaterial. I will provide you an intellectual basis for developing certain attitudes. If you are spiritual, the effects will only be enhanced.

First, you must accept that all events are learning opportunities designed for your growth. You need to understand that there are multiple forces and elements that cause any event. Therefore, it is necessary to develop an attitude that reflects that any event (good or bad) is not your fault. Events, whether desired or not, have two causes-: One is an obvious cause and other is an obscure cause. An obvious reason for an event where the electricity to your home is cut off might be a failure to make a monthly payment. If you are fired from your job, some obvious reasons for this might be a failure to perform or a breach of contract. Other events such as natural disasters, a divorce, or even getting a traffic ticket often have obvious causes.

Obscure causes are generally unknown to you. You do not have any say in these causes. These events are nature's way of correcting imbalances in personal, societal, or national structures. Some people may accept this truth under the Law of Karma, some may call it destiny, and some call it God's divine providence. Let's say a hurricane damages your house, and you are determined to fix it, but the house is beyond repair. How much control do you have over this event? You don't get to choose whether or not your house is condemned. The 2008-2009 financial crisis in the United States is an example of an event concerning a nation's Karma. A more obscure cause of this economic meltdown was likely nature seeking to correct an imbalance. Whether you place the blame on one group or another, you personally have no control over this monumental event.

The point I am trying to make is that is that there are certain events or forces that are not, and will never be, under your control. In these instances, your choice of action will be very limited or even non-existent. Blaming yourself is not only pointless, it will make matters even worse. Since the future is unknown, we cannot pinpoint the purpose of the event. It may well be that it is meant for our larger good. Sometimes nature forces a change upon us when we are reluctant to accept it on our own. The loss of a job or a sudden relocation may push you toward a new business adventure or into a new group of friends.

These events also force us to look at our lives from a different perspective. A financial disaster is a major event in anyone's life. It does not happen often, but if it does happen to you, you'll want to review and analyze all aspects of your life –

BOOMERANG

from your relationship with your spouse and children to your material attachments. There may be something in your life that is in need of readjustment, whether business, employment situation, social relations, family structure, economic conditions, or other areas.

If you find something that needs to be recalibrated, you are a good analyst and observer. Make the necessary adjustments quickly. It is possible that the ill effects you have been experiencing will go away or that their impact will be reduced. When a change is required and we fail to adopt that change, nature will force a circumstance upon us that we cannot overcome without embracing the needed change.

Know that everything happens for a reason, even tragic events such as divorce, emotional breakup, or death. It is important to acknowledge that Karma has played its part; it is indispensable to bring about necessary changes in your life. Therefore, there is no need for self-regret and where there is no self-regret, there will be no stress.

You might, at this point, be feeling like a victim of Karma. "Why me?" is the most common question I hear asked in a difficult situation. I wish the answer could be as easy as 1 + 1 = 2. There are always plenty of reasons why you think you *don't* deserve whatever you're suffering. There are also plenty of people to lay the blame on. Yet, these things will not explain why you were selected as the victim of this unfortunate event.

That is because the question cannot be answered using worldly insight.

One life continues in different bodies with multiple relationships, therefore, it is nature's secret why you were chosen. In the same breath, I hasten to add that there is always a second side to the Karmic coin. While you may be focused on the negative side, at the same time there is a positive side that will bring about benefits in the long term. Your best course of action is not to ask "Why me?" but to ask yourself, "What can I do now?" or "How can I benefit positively?"

With peace,

Purandar

P.S. Many people have asked me, "Can I dissolve or escape my Karma?" The practical answer to this question is "No." However, there is an extremely rare possibility for this to occur. A highly evolved person who has achieved mastery over energy, time, and space or can exert control over the five natural elements can transmute, transfer, or release their Karmic energy. However, it is highly unlikely that such a person will choose to interfere with the happenings of natural events, since their knowledge has transcended to a higher plane. In the case of the average person, a strong, emotionally-charged, faithful prayer might bring about divine help concerning your Karma.

Points to Remember

If an event causes you stress:

- Know that you are not at fault.
- Know that you did not and do not have control over it.
- Know that the present stress is momentary, and the full impact of the event is unknown at this moment.
- Know that you are just playing your part in the drama.
- Know that your best solution is to be a witness without being involved in thinking or judging the process.
- Know that a change is coming for the betterment of all concerned.

My Notes

8

BODY TO BODY

May 10, 2013

Dear Uma,

Do you see a cloud in a drop of dew that is resting on a leaf? Did you notice a tree in a piece of paper? I am sure that you have never noticed the oil that made the plastic in your cell phone! All these elements exist in the processes of creation, continuation, destruction, and rejuvenation. As you may realize, the forms that you perceive today are only one spot in its continuation in the process. Similarly, reincarnation is nothing but the continuing process of Karmic energy; it is a work in progress that is contributing to your own evolution. This process will continue to progress, whether you like it or not.

The word reincarnation raises many eyebrows. Many discard the notion immediately. Yet there is no better explanation for what you are now, and what you will become tomorrow, than the law of reincarnation – the Karma Principle.

As we have established previously, your Karmic energy does not dissolve upon your death. Since this energy is alive, intelligent, and capable of creating, a new body is created for that energy so that it can continue its experiences and, ultimately, be transformed. How, what, when, and where it happens is another mystery whose answer can only be found in the realm of all-knowingness.

Reincarnation, simply stated, is that when your present body is not suitable for your further evolution, your soul gives up its present body and enters into or creates another body, carrying the mental body along with it. The mental body consists of your thoughts, habits, memories, opinions, desires, etc. Practically anything that has gone through your mind and has not been transformed or transmuted. (Realize that this includes what has passed through your mind in this life and in all of your previous lives.) All of these elements are specks of energy that surround your physical body in their lighted forms. Together, these specks of energy and their light form the mental body that surrounds you. The radiance of the mental body depends on the intensity of each speck of energy and the amount of time that was devoted to it during any particular lifetime.

The mental body survives because its constituents are bits of energy, which cannot be destroyed.

Everybody agrees on the death of the physical body, but many differ on what happens to the soul – the living element in your body that makes you alive – before and after the death. The persons arguing against reincarnation must agree that energy cannot be destroyed; science tells us that it can be transformed, but it cannot be eliminated. So what happens to our mental body – which is made up of energy – when the physical body has died? Will it dissolve into universal space or consciousness, as some claim? Many opponents of reincarnation claim that there is no vehicle to carry or bind such energies, so they must dissolve. These individuals, however, forget that the living energy of the soul (a.k.a. consciousness) is ever existent and cannot be dissolved, even with the death of the physical body. Because of its magnetic properties, the mental body holds together and surrounds your soul.

The existence of this mental body forces the effects of Karma to take another physical form. The mental body is even more powerful than the physical body. You have millions and millions of thoughts, memories, that are stored up in the mental body. When you have shed your physical body, your mental body, enveloping your soul, causes the creation of a new body to form in the image of itself. (Remember, thought creates form!) At the time of that body's creation, it is the

Karma still existing – and the fruits of that Karma that have yet to be delivered – that are responsible for this process of reincarnation.

The Knower – or God, if you prefer – must see that you receive the fruits of your actions. As we explored in the previous letters, this requires the Knower to precisely coordinate time, place, instruments, and results. Because this involves such intricate organization, not all Karma can be fulfilled at the same time. A main reason for this is the vast number of persons (instruments) necessary in delivering the Karma. Because the crossing of these individuals and their paths must be coordinated, some memories are activated before others. When this occurs, the Karma of these memories is fulfilled when this certain group of people meets.

Because duality is the inherent nature of creation, the laws that bind you also have opposite laws that can be used to release you. The more you understand about the binding process, the more will be able to learn about the unbinding process.

Karmic law operates because of the magnetic nature of energy. Thoughts, being made up of energy, have magnetic properties. The Earth also has magnetic properties. The magnetic properties of Karma and Earth combine to produce a vehicle (the physical body, which is provided by the Earth) for the soul to come down to the Earth. You have no power to disconnect the magnetic properties of the Earth, but you can impact the energy on the other end of this equation. In order to do this, you must first understand the magnetic properties at work in your mental body. Magnetic properties are commonly manifested as attachments. A cycle of attachment is created when we take doer-ship or ownership of our actions, or when we begin to expect a certain outcome based on what we have done.

When you refuse to indulge in creating expectations for the fruits of your efforts, a parallel force emerges within the mental body. The easiest way not to have such expectations is to realize that you are merely an instrument in a complex set up of divine "happenings" where you have no choice but to participate (even though you might prefer to avoid participation). The vast majority of the population either lacks the mental capacity to disown their Karma or they have no desire to let go of the fruits of their karma. Yet, when you release your expectations and let go of the fruits of your actions, they no longer have power over you, because they cannot attach to your mind.

Now consider this: It is your *expectations*, more than the results, that trigger your emotional reaction to any given event. For example, if the result of an action is not in line with your expectations, you will be disappointed or even sad. If the result exceeds your expectations, you will be overjoyed. Therefore, you are choosing either joy or grief. But when you detach yourself from the result of any given action, it will not grieve you no matter the outcome.

Detachment is the opposite of attachment. Detaching yourself from the results of your actions, come what may, will not grieve you since you did not expect any particular outcome. If the result is just what you need – or even more – you will be happy. Know that such detachment does not arise in your mind unless your heart is peaceful and equanimity is established. You might be thinking, "Easier said than done," and you're right. Just know that a deep understanding of the laws that govern our existence will help you to establish these virtues.

You need to develop thinking patterns that travel along the following lines:

- The fruits of my actions will be given to me at the appropriate time (even if I don't know when that may be).
- I can't foresee the events of the future.
- What is going to happen will happen; I cannot control it. I cannot know what is best for me because I only have access to limited information.
- My actions affect not only me but the entirety of humanity.

- Everything is temporary and will be destroyed in due time, so what is the point in grief?

Honest, intense, and heartfelt belief in "Happening" (i.e. you are not the doer, but an instrument), and refusing to give in to expectations regarding the fruit of your actions (disconnecting the magnetic properties) dissolves the energies that fuel the cycle of reincarnation. Irrespective of when, where, and how you receive the results of your Karma, you are at least breaking the chain of endless birth and death.

There is another way to break the cycle. Consider this analogy: Imagine there is a dark room – pitch black. Nothing can be seen. Then, there is a dim light from a small lamp. Vague shapes emerge, barely visible in the faint light. Now, the room is flooded with light from a bright light bulb overhead. Everything is visible. The light of the small lamp remains on, but it has merged into the greater light of the overhead light bulb. At this point, you cannot find the point of separation between these two lights. Next, a person walks into the room and opens the curtains and windows. As it is the middle of the day and the room is flooded with broad daylight. The sun is shining into the room through each open window. The light of the small lamp, along with the light of the overhead light bulb, has now coalesced with the sunlight. In short, the weaker light merges with the stronger light, while the stronger light spreads out into the weaker light.

As we discussed earlier, memories (thoughts) are particles of light. The strength of that light depends upon the intensity of the experience and the resilience of the attachment. These lights (memories) are survived by the strength of the ego. Our soul is superior to the ego, so the light of the soul is the strongest. The light of the soul, when projected upon these particles of light (thoughts/memories), consumes them in its power. In short, the light of the soul can dissolve Karmic energies when projected upon them.

To achieve this, you need to concentrate on your heart center, which is the seat of the soul. It requires some practice to identify the movement or feelings of divine light in the heart center. Once you reach this point, you then project that divine light outside of your body and bring the thoughts you want to dissolve into your awareness. The intensity or the strength of your encounter with your soul, along with your concurrent awareness of thoughts and memories to be dissolved will determine your results.

In peace, with you,

Purandar

Points to Remember

- What you are experiencing is the consequence of what you have done in the past.
- What you think, say, feel and do today are the planted seeds you will reap in the future.
- It is not easy to break past Karma, but your soul can do it. It takes time, patience, and extreme devotion.
- Worrying about past Karma is the same as planting seeds for a bad future.

<u>My Notes</u>

9

HAPPENING

February 16, 2014

Dear Uma,

Does the ocean grieve when its waters are lost to the sun? Does the tree cry when a leaf falls? Do streams regret the loss of their identities when merging to become rivers? A lonely man on a garden bench reminds me of lost relationships. A beggar paints a picture of lost wealth and security. A patient in a hospital bed symbolizes lost hope and vitality. There is a news report that crosses my TV screen telling the story of a father who committed suicide, leaving behind three young daughters, because he could not repay his debt to a loan shark. Then I hear the joyous sounds of music and celebration, so I look out my window. Friends and family gather to wish a student well at her graduation party. Down the street, church bells are ringing. Perhaps the churchgoers are petitioning God to help us out. My mind drifts away from these sound and activities, as I ponder how all of these contradicting events can exist in the same moment. It makes me wonder about the amazing variety of "happenings" that make up our existence.

Remember that most of the issues that you face are located in the mind. They are thoughts, concepts, or beliefs systems – mind conditioning. You may have a number of belief systems. Some of the most common are:

- You need to have a certain amount of money to be happy
- You need to meet the expectations others have for you to win their approval
- You need to have a big house and an important job to be successful
- You must be in perfect health in order to be attractive to others

These are burdens you have placed upon yourself. These are your own desires, expectations and boundaries that you have set but are not meeting. These are failures of your own creation. You must be ready to give up your belief systems if you want to move on to a happier life.

Earlier, we examined the structure of the mind and the principles of Karma. Remember that all Karma is group

Karma. And if all Karma is group Karma, then it follows that all events happen according to the Karma of all persons involved that will best fit within the time, space, and actor's circumstances, as orchestrated by the Knower (read: God). Some call this "destiny;" others call it a "happening." A happening is inevitable, irrespective of your efforts and intentions. The happening principle can be summed up as follows: What has happened was supposed to happen; what is happening is supposed to be happening; what is supposed to happen will happen.

Under this principle, you are simply playing your part in life as an actor would in a drama. At this point, many of you will stop and say, "No, it is my desire or intention or will that guides my decisions; I do whatever I want to do." This brings up the eternal struggles of free will vs. destiny and self-effort vs. divine will. Personally – after many struggles and experiences – I have arrived at a position that does not support the idea of free will (though it has taken much time and fine-tuning to deeply understand this).

Many have asked, "If we have no free will and can exert no influence through our self-effort, how can we progress in life or obtain self-realization?" But this question presupposes that everything happens – or can happen – according to your self-efforts. Take a look back on your life and you will find that your self-effort, even your free will, did not always yield the results you desired. An argument that favors the idea of destiny relies on the principles of Karma to make its point. If all Karma is group Karma, then the result must also be a group result. The infinity of the group as a whole requires that all the instruments – including you – must function in synchronization, leaving no chance to individual choice.

So does this mean that free will is an illusion? Are we all merely toys left helpless in the hands of a superpower? What you consider to be your own intention or will, which resulted in a particular deed, was also part of a group intention or will, though this truth is not known to you. A divine will is needed to ensure that each instrument (individual being) plays their necessary part in a certain way. So how does it happen that divine will becomes our own will? We know that all deeds were first thoughts, and all thoughts are forms of light. The divine will extend a beam of light toward you, and when it hits you, in that split-second, your ego receives it and accepts it as its own thought. This process is so subtle and rapid that it escapes your worldly awareness, and you never perceive it as the divine will descending upon you. Your ego takes ownership of the divine will, and it is that ownership that creates your Karma.

If then, your thoughts and actions – and your Karma – are given to you by the divine will, the next question is: How can you progress along your path to self-realization? If your destiny operates as a result of the divine will, then it stands to reason that your progress must also be predestined. According to the principle of evolution, you are evolving every moment whether you are making an effort or not. Even if you are doing nothing, it must be a part of the process. (In fact, "doing nothing" is also "doing something." Doing something must also become doing nothing as part of the process.)

For most persons "Doing something" means some physical or mental activity, Similarly "Doing Nothing" means absence of the activity. However, when you are doing these activities, when you see them as part of "Happening", you are not doing it. The reverse is also true. when you consider "Doing nothing" you are removing your ownership or doer-ship in of the moment. Essentially you have become a participant of whatever is happening without binding yourself to the doing. This contradiction is not easy to comprehend. Absent the ego, there is no distinction between self-effort and divine will. When you have "no effort" you have no regrets for not reaping the fruit of your action.

Am I a toy in the hands of the divine? As long as your ego exists in your life, you may feel as though you are a toy (even though you will continue to regard each action, effort, and decision as "mine"). When the ego is gone, you will no longer view yourself as separate from the divine. It is then that the divine will become your will, too. If, in fact, you are *not* separate from the divine, then how does the question of free will come into play?

Consider this: You are supposed to be reading this writing; you would not be reading it unless it was meant for you. What has happened was supposed to happen, what is happening is supposed to be happening, and what is supposed to happen will happen.

Take the time to digest this principle completely. You will not have any regrets for what you did, as you are neither the judge nor the doer. You will not have any disappointments for what did not happen, as you had no expectations. You will not have any worry or fear, since you have no control over the future. Outwardly, you are an actor in a drama; inwardly, you are an observer.

With peace,

Purandar

P.S. The happening principle never stops you from taking the required actions or laying the necessary plans for your future; all it requires is for you to accept the present moment as it is, without worrying about the future or lamenting over the past. When you accept the happening principle, your body is viewed as nothing more than a performing instrument and you are separate from it.

When you observe yourself from this perspective you might be amazed to find that you view your problems differently when looking at them from the outside. When you can separate yourself from the problem, you can begin to judge yourself (and your actions) honestly.

Points to Remember

- It is necessary to understand the principle of "happening" in order to remove guilt, self-deprecation, and judgment from your life.
- Know that everything happens in its own time and place.
- Realize and accept that you are not responsible for what has happened or will happen.
- Know that you will do whatever you are supposed to do at the proper time – not a moment earlier or later.

My Notes

10

DEVILS IN THE DEN

April 27, 2014

Dear Uma,

Good morning! It is a beautiful spring morning. Flowers are rushing to bloom, the sun is pouring out abundant light, and the sky is decorated with the occasional cloud. What feelings do you have? Do your thoughts follow your emotions or vice versa? Can you see how your thoughts and emotions are intertwined?

In stressful situations – such as a divorce, a foreclosure, or an illness – emotions run high. It is negative emotions that cause you stress. Fear is the strongest negative emotion. So what is fear? When you examine it, you will find it is nothing more than a thought. Being a thought, fear has all the inherent attributes of thoughts. For our purposes, we will focus on the magnetic property of thoughts and the creative capacity of thoughts.

The magnetic property of thoughts operates in much the same way as the law of attraction – like attracts like. The more you focus on negative emotions or fears, the more likely you are to build upon these negative thoughts by attracting more negativity. The creative capacity of thoughts functions in a similar way, in that a focus on negativity will ultimately bring you more negativity. Time being the vehicle of thoughts, more time you spend thinking about your fears, more likely to materialize. In this way, you are your own worst enemy; you end up manifesting the thing you are afraid of. Fear produces a negative feeling regarding an anticipation that something will or won't happen in the future. So it is these fearful expectations that cause your worries. Of course, whether your fear comes to pass or not depends on a multitude of factors. Most of these factors are beyond your control, and even beyond the scope of your comprehension. So why would you stew over a matter that you have no control over?

Let us examine some of the most common fears we face today:

Future Fears

Your employer's business is struggling. You have heard rumors that they may be filing for bankruptcy. A lot of employees have been laid off recently, and you fear that you may be next. Or maybe you own a business that is failing to generate enough income to pay all your bills. Your cash balances are very low, and you've maxed out your credit. You fear that your business might fail.

The first thing you must do when facing fears of the future is to calm yourself down. Remember to be in the present. Though you may think it likely that you will lose your job or your business, it is still something in the future. Today, you have shelter and food on your table. Something may or may not happen tomorrow, but it is not happening today. It is wise to realize that you have no control over the future. You also have no way of knowing what will or won't happen. Forget your fears of the future. Concentrate on what you have today, right now, at this moment. Today you have what you need. Tomorrow, at best, is still uncertain. Perhaps your company will get a new loan or win a fresh contract. Maybe your hours will be cut, but you will still keep your job. Someone who is interested in your work may offer to buy your business from you, or you may find a new service to offer that will bring in more revenue.

Today is peaceful and uneventful. Remember yourself as a tiny child, carefree and full of wonder. Become childlike again. Never worry about tomorrow. This is the key to happiness. Take each moment as it comes. Let yourself be occupied with the present moment, not focused on being concerned about the next moment. You might be thinking, "How can I do that? It's so irresponsible!" The answer is simple: You are not responsible for your circumstances or the events that shape your life; you do not have control over any of it. Thinking about the next moment – the future – is nothing more than an invitation for worries.

Know that whatever you have in the present moment is what you are supposed to have; whatever situation you are facing, it is for your own good. If you focus on what the present moment is, and on what needs to be done right in this moment, there will be no room for worries or fears. I cannot emphasize this point strongly enough. If you can accept this truth and engrain it as deeply as possible into your very being, then you will have incredible peace forever. This is the ultimate key to removing your fears and worries. The present moment IS, and what is needed to be done right at this moment, not in next moment.

Past Fears

In the past, you were unable to make your mortgage payment, so your house was foreclosed on. Now, you are fearful that any change in your income will lead to the same kind of situation. You are constantly worried that you will be kicked out of your home, with nowhere to go. Even in times of crisis, remember that duality is the inherent nature of creation. This means that there is an equal amount of positive news that will come from your current situation, even though you are overcome with the negative. This perspective may not be visible to you in the moment, but when you look back on your life, you will see that many good things have come from seemingly bad situations.

Even if you were to experience another foreclosure, consider these possibilities:

- You now have an opportunity to find the work you love to do.
- You now have the opportunity to move to a more affordable property.
- You can move to a new location – somewhere you've always wanted to live.
- You have an opportunity to restructure your life and your finances.
- Now that you are no longer tied down, you may have more opportunity to spend time with friends and family, or maybe you now have the freedom to travel.
- Nature is forcing a change on you in order to release you from binding circumstances.

Many times, unfortunate circumstances indicate that you need to change. Most people are resistant to change, and even more reluctant to make those changes themselves. It is because of this very stubbornness that these seemingly negative circumstances are forced upon you – to cause you to make a change. Change is inevitable; nothing stays the same.

Confusion prevails in such times of transition. The present has not become the past, and the future is waiting to come. Let go of the present quickly. There is always a sunrise after a sunset. Focus on the moment, live in the present, and remain positive.

Imaginative Fears

Imaginative fears are not based on past troubles or future outcomes. They are purely the work of your imagination and they result from your worldly attachments. It is easy to imagine a terrible scenario, such as all your savings being swindled from you. You could spend your time complaining about all the things that are wrong with your car, rather than being thankful that you have one at all. All of these imaginings arise from your attachments.

When you were born, you came into the world empty-handed. When you leave the world, you will go out empty-handed. When you die, you will not only lose your body, but your home, your possessions, and all other assets, too. Here is the truth: everything is temporary. All of your possessions – your house, your car, your keepsakes, even this book – are temporary. The universe is constantly changing – nothing remains the same. Whatever you lose today will eventually return to you (perhaps in another form) if you keep your thoughts positive. Negative thoughts produce negative energy, and positive thoughts produce positive energy. Tell your mind that whatever you are experiencing is a temporary phase. The trick is to pass through it carefully and peacefully.

Relational Fears

Relational troubles, such as a divorce or a broken relationship, are issues of the heart. In these cases, the heart prevails over intelligence. The unfortunate truth is that all relationships are temporary, no matter how deeply you are attached. Because your love exists within the constraints of time and space, what you believe to be love is actually a scenario arising from your conditioned mind. If you have any requirements in a relationship, then that relationship is not based on love, but on expectations. This is why so many relationships are fraught with jealousy, disappointment, and betrayal. No matter how reasonable and right you believe your conditions are, know that they will all change, for better or worse, eventually. It is only the day-to-day relationship built on self-sacrifice, respect, reverence, faith, and devotion, with no demand of reward or expectation of reciprocation, that is a true reflection of love. Take a look at your own relationships; do they measure up against this standard? Or are you wrapping the other person up in expectations and demands?

If your relationship passes this comparison test, then you are the gem of humanity. There is no divorce in your future. If you did not pass the test, then seriously examine the areas where you may have created a temporary arrangement by establishing conditions, expectations, or reciprocal demands. These days, all relationships start with expectations, hopes, and conditions. The one thing these arrangements have in common is that they will all eventually fail (although some will stay in a relationship for financial, familial, or social reasons; a long -lasting relationship may not be an indication of love as much as it is a sign that the individuals involved have learned to live together and tolerate each other). All broken relationships produce pain and suffering. Hurts of the heart are difficult to heal and may take a long time to mend. So what can you do to heal your heart and begin to practice true love in your relationships?

First and foremost, you must stop trying to find fault with others. Have you ever heard of the saying, "An eye for an eye?" When you are overcome with anger and the desire to get even with someone, it is a clear sign that your ego has taken over. Forget this tit-for-tat approach. You must let go of your anger and disappointment, which are solely comprised of negative energy. When you unleash your anger on others, like a boomerang; it will come back upon your head, hurting you further. Remember the principles of resonance and reflection. For the sake of your own peace, do not dwell on thoughts of revenge. As we learned earlier, such negative energy can manifest in many other areas (health, finances, relationships, etc.) and cause you great heartache. If you take a moment to watch your ego, knowing that it is fueling your negative feelings, it will begin to dissolve under the weight of your awareness.

The next step is to forgive. If you have trouble forgiving, think about this: If you were in the other person's shoes, with the same level of intelligence and mental functioning, the same life experiences, and the same level of consciousness, you would have acted exactly the same way. With the proper concentration and a heartfelt approach, you will find that a feeling of compassion will arise toward this other person. It is from this state that you can truly let go of your feelings and forgive.

You must also ask the other party for forgiveness, whether you consider yourself to be at fault or not. If you feel reluctant to do this, then that your ego is rising up again. Remember that your goal here is not to judge who is at fault. By simply asking for forgiveness – even for faults or mistakes you may have attributed to the other person – you will often find that the other person will calm down as well. This happens because you are sending out peaceful and compassionate energies that will resonate within the other person. And, just as with negative energy, this positive energy will attract like energy and bring it back to you. If you feel peace at the end of the exercise, you have succeeded.

Do your best to remind yourself that all events happen according to Karma and destiny. If you can learn to accept events – both positive and negative – as they come, without anger or fear, you will find peace. And it is from this place of peace and true surrender that you will find solutions to your problems.

Many people refuse to let go of their anger or fantasies of revenge because they have a fear of losing face. They are afraid that their friends and family – even the world in general – will look down upon them. This fear shows a lack of self-confidence and is a clear manipulation of the ego. Remember the following: (1) All persons face these kinds of difficulties in their lives. (2) What is happening is not within your control. (3) It is nobody else's business to judge you based on your current circumstances. In reality, it is the most trying of circumstances that will reveal who your true allies are, from among your friends and relatives. If your friends and relatives have no compassion on you, or if they lack consideration for your present circumstances, then you need to reevaluate your relationships.

When you are facing fears of all kinds, sit down and write each fear out on a separate piece of paper. Then write out your responses to that fear. Ask yourself, "What is the worst thing that can happen if my fear materializes?" Write a second question "Is this result the end of the world?" Invariably, your answer will be a resounding, "No."

Count your blessings. You are alive. You are capable of change. And no problem is too big for you to tackle. The future is always uncertain, at best. If you cannot know the future, and you cannot control it, then why should you waste your time worrying about it? Remember, the more time you spend worrying about your fears, the more likely they are to manifest and bring you misery. Expose your fearful thoughts to the light of your soul. Bring your fear into your awareness, and it will go away. If your fears sneak back in, drag them before your awareness again. Each time you do this, your fear will become less and less powerful until it will finally disappear.

With peace,

Purandar

P.S. The Oneness Principle of the universe states that there is no "other." Fear comes from the "other", not from you. When there is no "other", where is the fear?

Points to Remember

- Know that you are not at fault. Circumstances do happen beyond your control.

- Don't think about the future; the future is always uncertain.

- All fears are imaginations that stem from thoughts of the future.

- Since the future is an mental illusion, what comes from it (your fears) is also an illusion.

- Live only in the present moment.

- There is a solution for every problem.

- Learn to love change. Change opens new doors.

<u>My Notes</u>

11

APPLES AND ORANGES

October 13, 2014

Dear Uma,

Clouds disperse only to become clouds again. Leaves fall only to become a source of nutrients for the tree that they fell from. The entirety of creation self-destructs in order to create again. So it is with desire. If you satisfy a desire, it will soon resurrect itself. Desire is a prime motivational force for most people. After all, the desire to possess the knowledge of good and evil was so strong that humanity is still learning the lesson.

Desires can be classified into three categories – natural, sensory, and Karmic. Natural desires are those desires whose satisfaction is necessary in order for us to continue our lives. These include the desire to drink water, the desire to eat food, and the desire for shelter. Sensory desires are not necessary to your survival, and can be resisted. For example, I may desire to have a glass of wine instead of milk, but I can choose not to. In either case, my survival is not at stake. Karmic desires are the ones that you have no control over; you will oblige them, no matter what. Some Karmic desires may appear to be sensory desires. However, these desires force you to act upon them, removing the element of choice.

Desires are normally given a bad name in the spiritual fields, but this is not a fully accurate depiction. Desires can lead you along a higher path or drag you down to destruction. Your ability to discern the nature of your desires can help lead you along the path to enlightenment; lack of discrimination in this area can only speed you on your way to destruction. Some desires arise from your memories. Others are divinely instituted. Some may be subtle or unknown to you, but they are strong nonetheless. Your desires can propel you to think, speak, and act in a particular way. Thoughts, words, and actions that result from your desires will obviously yield results, but they may not appear in the way you expect. The outcome of your desires depends on the nature of the desire you have acted on at the time, place, and in the manner anticipated by you. Therefore the fruit of your desires can cause you frustration, disappointment, and grief, or peace. The desired fruit of your actions may be what you want, but not what you need.

You should be careful to distinguish between what you need and what you want. Remember earlier when I said that I might have a desire for a glass of water or a glass of wine? The first desire might be a need, while the second could be a want. Wants are our wishful desires. So, how can you tell the difference? The answer is simple: if you do not have the thing you desire in the present moment, then it is safe to say that you do not need it.

It is a common spiritual belief that a person's needs will be satisfied. So what are your genuine needs in the present moment, besides oxygen? There are physical needs, such as food and water, and then there are spiritual needs. Your most genuine needs are those that will lead to your spiritual uplifting. You may be starving at this moment, but it does not mean you need food. Perhaps your genuine need may be to realize and understand the pangs of the hungry and starving. Whatever you consider to be your needs may or may not be what you actually need for the present moment. Consider the case of a homeless man. By most worldly standards, we would say that he needs a home. However, if he is currently in the process of learning a valuable and necessary life lesson, then it is not a home that he needs. He will have a home when that home is justified, or when it is necessary for his personal evolution. In other words, if something is not necessary for your personal evolution then it is not really a need. This is a hard ideology to reconcile with the modern thinking of our society.

If you are losing your home, your job, or a relationship, then know that such an occurrence is necessary. I have seen scores of incidents where the loss of a job leads someone to strike out in a new profession or to start their own business. Losing one's home is deemed a terribly unfortunate event when it occurs, but homelessness can teach a person the importance of community and charity. All such devastating occurrences may cause a person to confront their ego, shed their pride, discover their true self, and eventually make them a free person. Though it is hard medicine to swallow, sometimes it is necessary for your own well-being.

It is your wants – not your needs – that will bring you misery, worries, and stress. Believe that your needs will be satisfied. This will allow you to be calm, patient, and loving. These feelings will project positive vibrations out into your surroundings. Others will be able to feel your tranquility and happiness reflected on them.

When spiritualists advise you to avoid desires, they are usually pointing the finger at "enjoyment desires." Desires create thoughts; thoughts create agitations; and agitations, in turn, require satisfaction. Satisfaction will create attachment, and attachments will create habits. And so the circle continues. All desires will lead you to perform tasks with expectations.

Tasks become the threads of memories- binding threads. The results of such tasks may or may not be in line with your expectations. So when you act from desire, expecting some kind of result, you will react either positively or negatively to the outcome. Maybe you will be disappointed when you fail to achieve satisfaction. Maybe you will be ecstatic that things turned out according to your plans. Whether you are disappointed or satisfied is largely dependent on your expectations of when and where you will see your results. It is, therefore, your expectations that rule your emotions. So, in order to be free from disappointment or apprehensions, you must do the opposite – do not expect results.

You might find it ridiculous that I would tell you to do something without expecting some kind of result. Well, this is what "reverse thinking" is all about – erasing your preconceived expectations and embracing a newer way of thinking (and existing.) Remember, you are not "doing" anything; you are just performing your part like an actor would in a play. Again, embracing this concept requires a reversal in your thinking.

So why is it necessary for you to stop creating expectations? When you expect a result, you are actually setting a limitation. Let's explore an example: Say you invest in a certain stock out of a desire to make money. Because of that desire, you have made an investment that you expect will be doubled. What your expectation has done is set a limit on your result. What if the stock could have tripled or quadrupled? When you do not expect anything, then you are not setting limits, so that the necessary result can be delivered. Whether you receive a huge return on your investment or no return at all, you will not be disappointed because you have expected nothing.

Does this then mean that you should stop performing tasks all together? Should you simply remain idle? By no means. You must do whatever is necessary to carry out your normal duties in the course of your life. But as you perform your daily tasks, you must also do so without expectations. You cannot expect that the results of your actions will appear in any particular manner, time, and place of your choosing. The law of Karma guarantees that you will receive the fruits of your actions. Do not let your wishful desires trap you in expectations. Expectations are the babies of desire. Therefore, watch what you desire. Remove your wants, and save yourself from grief! Easier said than done! Begin, at least, with more easily disposable wants and you'll see the benefits mentally, spiritually and financially.

As I said earlier, your desires will also create attachments. These attachments could be to material things (such as a house or a car) or to people (your spouse, your children, etc.). Assume, for a second that you do not have anything; no spouse, no home, no money, no job – nothing. You will realize that when you have nothing, you do not have to defend or care for anything. You do not have to worry about satisfying your desires or expectations. You can move and live anywhere you like, pick up any job that you choose, and sleep anywhere without risking or losing anything. Nobody can order you to do anything. You don't have to justify yourself to anyone. Swami Vivekananda stated, "He is the happiest who has nobody to love." (I am sure by "love" he meant "attachment," in a worldly sense.)

Realize that most of the attachments you have are based on sensory desires, which arise out of the societal conditioning of your mind. If you think of your attachments as constraints on your freedom, you will realize that many of your problems stem from your expectations regarding those attachments. The problems start when we begin to imagine that we have to have "something," or that we need to satisfy the expectations of our friends, relatives, etc. If these things are not needed in order to take you along your higher path, then they are wishful desires and will cause you more harm than good. It will actually block good from coming to you.

When you expect things to be a certain way, this is the first sign of such a blockage. We judge persons, events, ideas, or anything else, within the framework of our mental conditioning. It blocks creativity, and it sets limits on your evolution. Know that deep-seated viewpoints, concepts, and thought forms also create desires.

Because desires are so strong, they can easily block out the changes that are needed in our lives. Add to this the fact that most people are apprehensive (to say the least) about any perceived or anticipated change, and you can understand why sometimes change must be forced upon us in order to compel us to alter our course. This is especially true when there is a desire or expectation that creates a conflict.

Know that nothing is constant – no condition, no circumstance, nothing you own and no relationship you have. The only constant is change, whether or not you are aware that it is occurring. Your awareness of change cannot speed it along nor slow it down.

Let me ask you a question: What were your viewpoints when you were a teenager? Did you hold beliefs then that are different from the ones you hold now? Your viewpoints are different because you have experienced change. In moments when you have had to make a major change (due to the loss of a relationship or a job, a need to relocate, etc.), did anything you do stop that change from happening? Were you able to remain exactly as you were? Change may be slow and smooth or sudden and dramatic, but it happens, and you have no control over it.

Change will come; it is a fact of nature. You must not only understand that change is constant and is coming, but you must also accept this fact in peace. Be patient with yourself,

126

and give yourself time to transition. A transitional time is necessary to prepare yourself and all the affected persons and to put everyone in the proper frame of mind. It is also necessary to prepare for the right time, at the right place. If you know change is coming, this will give you some hope and solace, but it can also elicit fears and shivers. If you are cooperating with the change, it will be smooth and easy. If you are resisting the change, it can be sudden and dramatic--even destructive. Be open to new ideas, contrary opinions, and beliefs. Be open and conscious of your viewpoints and thinking patterns. The rules of the world change according to time and space. The laws of moralities change from country to country. What was right some time ago is wrong now.

It is not just your own desires that may be exerting influence on your life. As we learned earlier, everything is comprised of energy. Take a look at your friends, relatives, coworkers, and other acquaintances. Peacefully observe each of these relationships individually. As you ponder these relationships, try to identify what each person expects of you. Some common expectations will involve your behavior, the amount of time you spend with them, your level of emotional involvement, and even your financial obligations to them. Each person's expectations toward you are based on their own desires. These desires have created expectations that have formed a cloud of energy they project toward you. Realize that you may be in several clouds, coming from several people, all carrying energies that may be in conflict. Other people's expectations and the energies that they create have affected you all your life. You may have experienced their effects at various times as confusion or internal dilemmas.

It is also important to note that you create similar clouds of energy that gravitate toward others based on your expectations for them. Your desire that someone will or won't think, speak, or act in a certain way will, in turn, create expectations of their behavior. When somebody 'hurts' you, know that it was not his or her word or behavior that hurt you, but the failures of your own expectations of others made you feel hurt. (In such a case, there is no need even to forgive the other). If you simply let go of the expectations you have attached to your various relationships, you will find your attitudes and feelings much improved, along with the state of each relationship. (You will have a chance to try this for yourself at the end of this chapter.)

When you are thinking, speaking, and acting in a manner that is without expectations, because you have let go of your desires toward another person, you will be able to act from your heart, without worries or stress. This freedom will also create a state of peace within and around you. This peace leaves no room for stress. This is a labor of love for peace.

I need to revisit the ego to make one more point. The ego and your desires have a parent-child relationship. A desire to have

128

a front row seat at a concert, for instance, is a statement of ego. This desire, which starts as a thought (which is fueled by the "mine and thine" comparison), quickly turns into a feeling. Ego's "mine and thine" mentality fuels your desires. Therefore ego is the original cause of your stress. Whenever you classify something as "mine," it is your ego talking. "My house," "My family," "My reputation," "My job," – these are all examples of ego-based thinking. Your stress comes from your assumed responsibility of ownership. Ownership creates a need for preservation and protection. The self preservation element of ego creates the worry. Worries are the imaginations of a future happening that has no basis or existence in the present. Since you have no control over the future, you must resist the efforts of the ego by releasing your desires and expectations.

My approach is to help you minimize the influence of your ego as much as possible, simply by being aware of it. You do not have to do anything else. Just by being aware of it, the ego will become less and less powerful. Even if you have a prominent ego, by practicing awareness, it will start to shrink, becoming more and more subtle. Later, it will begin to hide in false humility, a show of inferiority, and self-proclamations devoid of ego. Take the example of a rich friend. He knows you live in a middle-class neighborhood. He lives in a mansion in a rich neighborhood. When he welcomes you to his estate and shows unwarranted humility, know that the ego is hiding.

Another example is a highly intelligent and knowledgeable expert who pretends to know nothing; this is an exhibition of false humility. With hidden humility, there is an underlying desire for other party to appreciate the person's wealth or wisdom. Be careful when your ego assumes a reverse cycle of inferiority; it becomes harder to detect at this point.

With peace,

Purandar

P.S. Sometimes I linger on certain topics (as if I have not already said enough). I know I am asking something that seems almost impossible. You may not be able to completely eliminate your desires, but at least try to reduce as many as possible. Watch them as they occur. Remove them with discrimination. A desire-less state is the most peaceful state of being.

Let me leave you with the following challenge: For the next month, let go of all the desires and expectations you have of the person closest to you. Observe the changes that take place in your thinking, in your reactions, and in your energy. If you experience peace and freedom, expand this experiment to include other relationships, one at a time. Even if you cannot let go of all your desires and expectations, just succeeding with the smallest of desires (those that seem least important) will surely change you. Your relationships will improve. You will experience less anxiety and more peace. You will feel a freedom that you have never experienced before.

Points to Remember

- Having no desires means having no need to satisfy; having no need to satisfy means no expectations; having no expectations means nothing can disappoint you.

- If you have no desires, you will have no requirements to fulfill; when you have no requirements to fulfill, you will not experience the stress that would accompany them.

- Having no desires translates into freedom from needs, expectations, requirements, and even the time limits that bind you. When you are free of these things, you will also be free of stress.

Exercises

Find a quiet place where you will not be disturbed. Calm your mental and physical bodies with deep breathing and relaxation. Now, find the three most intense desires of your being. (If you can imagine a genie standing before you, waiting to grant you three wishes, what would you ask for?)

Focus on your most intense desire first. Be aware of it. Bring all the thoughts, imaginings, and expectations you have created concerning this desire into your awareness. Now turn your attention to your heart center, with no other thought in mind. Mentally commit with full intensity, and without any hesitation, to let go of this desire. (Your intensity and emotions are most important to be effective).

See (or imagine) white, silvery lights coming out of your heart center, spreading out to cover your desire and all the thoughts, imaginings, and expectations connected with it. Keep these things firmly within the light until all images and thoughts of such desires disappear, along with your desire.

In light, darkness vanishes.

Repeat the same process for your two remaining desires. Practice this exercise every day for a few days, until you feel no emotions concerning your three deepest desires. In the end, you will feel light and peaceful, as if a burden has been lifted from you.

Upon completion of above exercise, make three lists. Title the first list "Have to Do," the second list, "Should Do," and the third list, "Must Do." List your top five priorities in each category. Once you have finished, repeat the first exercise for each item.

Before going to bed, spend some time pondering the following concepts so that you can fall asleep with these thoughts in your mind:

- A state that is free from desires is the most peaceful state.

- Having no desires means you have no requirements to fulfill; having no requirements to fulfill means you have no stress arising from the need to comply.

- Having no desires means—having no time limits to bind you. Having no needs means you have no expectations; having no expectations means not waiting for anything; when you are not waiting for anything, you cannot be disappointed.

- Having no desires, needs, expectations, or requirements means you have all the time you need. No time limits apply to you; this means you will not need to rush in life, so you will not feel needless stress.

- Desirelessness will set you free. Meditate on this truth until you realize the "how" and "why," of each of your major, unfulfilled desires. Then accept it as your own truth.

My Notes

12

BALANCE

May 24, 2014

Dear Uma,

Today's subject matter is very important to your peace of mind. The vast majority of humankind will either be completely lost or will shut themselves down when they hear the word "duality." Even monks and spiritualists do not fully grasp the depths of this principle; they simply consider it to be a part of creation and nothing more. Yet, there is infinitely more to be learned from the principle of duality, especially as it pertains to our pursuit of equanimity. Most individuals consider duality to be insurmountable. But even Mount Everest seemed unconquerable until Tenzing Norgay and Edmund Hillary stepped foot on the summit. I ask only that you try to stay with me as I discuss this principle.

The function of duality is to acknowledge the opposite and to maintain a balance between the two, hence the concept of equanimity. Simply stated, duality is a relationship between two opposing and equal elements. Some examples of this include hot and cold, male and female genders, positive and negative charges, the emotions of love and hate, etc. The existence of duality allows us to perceive and live in this world. How do you think "hot" would feel if you had never experienced "cold?" Would you know what true happiness felt like without knowing the depths of sorrow? These contradictions are part of our daily lives and are the ways in which we grow and learn. In our quest for the peace, the principle of duality tells us to acknowledge that there is an equal amount of opposite for whatever exists in the same time and space. Therefore, if you are agitated, according to the principle of duality, there also exists an equal amount of peace. But it is only in the midst of disturbance that you find yourself craving peace. If somebody hates you, it is the negative form of love. If you are worried or stressed out, you can choose to be stress-free since an equal amount of peace is available to you in the moment.

Think of duality as an atom of energy; that is everywhere in the universe. This "atom" contains positive and negative particles. In its original state, it has equal amount of positive and negative particles and is considered neutral. When it comes in contact with a form or an emotion or a thought, it becomes positive or negative depending upon the energy of such contact. Yet even if the "atom" is considered positive or negative, it still contains both positive and negative particles. This "atom" is the basic element of creation. In our earlier discussion of the mind, we noticed that our minds are conditioned. This conditioning is often paired in opposites, such as love and hate, anger and peace, desire and distaste, etc. Your conditionings lead you to make judgments about virtually everything. If you look back on a memory you have of an event or an encounter from your past, you will find that you have formed a positive or negative opinion about it. You carry this opinion (and its positive or negative energy) with you, and its presence further solidifies your mental conditioning. Whether this opinion is positive or negative, the principle of duality states that there is a latent amount of opposite energy attached to this opinion. Just as an atom contains both positive and negative particles, your opinions create opposite energy as well. Even the strongest opinions you hold and the most intense emotions you feel have an opposite amount of accumulated energy waiting to be unleashed.

While duality refers to the contrasting relationship between two elements, equanimity is concerned with the balancing of these elements. When the opposing forces of duality are equal in strength, they are in a state of equanimity, which neutralizes the effects of both. Remember our discussion of the atom? When an atom contains the same amount of positive and negative particles, its charge is said to be neutral. This idea of neutrality is central to our understanding of equanimity.

Most people will see equanimity as an unattainable ideal, and therefore, discard it and its pursuit as frivolous. Know that we are aiming for the mountain top while the vast majority of humanity still lives in the foothills, refusing to climb for fear of falling. I will first attempt to explain this principle clearly in a way you can understand. The most common definition of equanimity is equal mindedness toward everything. Being able to maintain this state of peace in any situation is the goal of this principle. The nature of equanimity rejects the classifications of "positive" or "negative" and maintains a state of neutrality.

What does this neutrality look like? A state of equanimity removes the conflict between the opposing forces of duality. For example, a person existing in equanimity has no likes or dislikes because they are neutral – neither positive nor negative. Equanimity rejects the ideas of "good" and "bad." After all, what might appear to be "bad" for one person could turn out to be "good." Similarly, what appears to be "good" for one person may be "bad" for another. These ideas of "good" and "bad" (or positive and negative) are completely subjective. That is because the classifications of "good" and "bad" depend largely on the judgments of the individual. As we discussed earlier, these judgments arise from the conditioning of your mind.

Our memories have conditioned our minds to react to the thoughts, emotions, events, and people we encounter. I would go so far as to say that we consider it our right to react to anything and everything. Again, you must reverse your thinking. It is not necessary for you to react to anything. But isn't it your nature as a human being to react? How can you refrain from reacting? You can do this very easily when you know, understand and accept that events are beyond your control, and any judgment you hold that would classify an event as bad or good is based solely on your limited and conditioned viewpoints. Because of the conditioning of the mind and the fact that any one person's knowledge will be understandably limited, it is likely that they will judge events imperfectly, as their decisions are made within a limited sphere of knowledge.

One of the most important factors in maintaining equanimity has to do with emotions. Everyone has emotions, but not everyone must remain a slave to them. Many people are ruled by their tumultuous emotions, which can lead to serious predicaments. For example, very strong, negative emotions can send you into a bout of depression. Depression is the ultimate trap, blinding you to any and all escape routes. It lowers your self-esteem, cuts you off from the outside world, and can even lead to suicidal thoughts. Emotions – both negative and positive – can cloud your judgment, causing thoughts, words, and actions that can affect your health, job performance, relationships, and so much more. Rather than being pulled in all directions by passing or conflicting emotions, the self-realized individual can master them by achieving equanimity.

In order to loosen the grip of emotions in your life, you must always remember that all feelings and circumstances are temporary. Everything can change in a day – or even a moment. Just as your judgments are imperfect, so are your emotions. You might feel very differently about a situation if you had all the information. What might appear to be "bad" to your limited viewpoint could easily cause you sadness or lead to feelings of hopelessness and depression. However, if you knew the breadth of the situation, and the future impact it will have on your life, you might feel different. Have you ever had someone give you "bad news" only to find that it has become "good news" a week or a month later? Every new moment brings change, so why allow your fleeting emotions over your present circumstances rule you when those circumstances are going to change?

Furthermore, you must realize that, despite your viewpoints and emotions, everything in creation is working together exactly as it must in order to bring things to their perfect end.

Remember the principle of happening? What was supposed to happen has happened, what is supposed to be happening is happening, and what is supposed to happen will happen. Therefore, whatever you have in the present moment – thoughts, feelings, relationships, circumstances, etc. – you are supposed to have them. There is nothing to be done but to accept the present moment "as it is." The idea that what you have now is what you are supposed to have in the present moment is not easy to accept. Everything happens for a reason, though that reason is unknown to us. This belief system requires both a strong conviction and a total surrender. Once you believe that everything is happening for a reason, it will become easier not to react (a habit of equanimity).

Another useful tool in the pursuit of equanimity is the changing of your viewpoints. As was said before, whether something is desirable or undesirable to you are based on your memories of past experiences. These memories have formed your viewpoints. This simply means that everything is now viewed and judged within the limits of your mind. If you change your viewpoints in some aspects of your life, you may be able to more easily identify the truth of your circumstances. For example, you may think that owning a large and illustrious home will be good for your reputation and your family. However, it may be that owning such a home will bankrupt you financially. Or perhaps you will have to work overtime in order to afford your mortgage payments, and do so at the expense of your familial relationships. It might be best for you to let go of the preconceived view that a larger or nicer home is better in order to salvage your finances or your family.

Many people find it difficult to give up a viewpoint. Their mental conditioning is so deeply ingrained that adjusting their perspective seems next to impossible. Maybe they have tunnel vision and are missing the forest for the trees. Maybe they are forcing everything to fit into their black and white viewpoint, failing to see that there are many shades in between. Very firm viewpoints, concepts, and beliefs are like rigid structures surrounding your physical body; they do not allow anything to come in or out. They are blockages that are creating obstacles to your personal development. If you think you might belong to one of these groups, do your best to seek outside counsel and behavioral feedback. Do not allow yourself to get stuck in a position that will undermine you. Know that your judgments are causing you pain and suffering.

Say you see your doctor for a routine check-up, and the doctor finds that that you have stomach cancer. Now, the fact that you have cancer is a reality. If you immediately judge the situation as "bad," you will easily succumb to worries and fears. This will do nothing but cause you stress and heartache, effectively multiplying the problem. In some cases, your fear may be so great that it immobilizes you. Yet by refusing to judge the situation or react emotionally to it, you will keep a clear head and be more easily able to navigate your path forward. Nothing you do in this moment will immediately change your diagnosis. However, you can ask your doctor's advice, discuss your next steps, get a second opinion, explore alternative treatments, etc. By maintaining equanimity even in the gravest of circumstances, you will find peace. Since the acceptance of this principle changes your energy patterns, you attract a similar kind of energy in terms of your relationships and circumstances.

Let me make myself clear: Accepting the present moment by surrendering to "what is," should not be confused with non-action. As in the above example, there are always things that you must do and actions you must take to continue functioning in society and in life. This idea has to do with 'Being' rather than reacting to whims of emotions. You will find peace only in 'Being'.

Take a moment to look into your past. Search out memories of life events that caused you to fight. These could be financial events, relationship troubles, or even emotional battles – the point is, you struggled. This was duality in action. You refused to accept what was and drew your battle lines. You fought and may have thought that you have won, at least by earthly standards. But in fighting, you lost peace. This happens again and again. Fighting is resisting what it is irrespective of its appropriateness. You may need to take right action or may not need to do anything, leaving everything as it is and waiting for the next moment to come. If you want to be free from these constant battles, you need to accept the principles herein at the deepest level and follow the path indicated, so that opposing forces are not triggered.

A common question I hear when discussing equanimity has to do with traditionally "positive" feelings and emotions. Some ask, "Am I not supposed to feel love, loyalty, joy or such other noble feelings?" Your goal is not to be an emotionless robot devoid of all feelings. Rather, your goal is to find peace. Know that equanimity brings peace. Peace makes room for true love, not attachment or lust. Love will bring you joy (or bliss). Love, joy, and peace are natural conditions of Being. It is a state of Being-ness rather than one of attempted doing. Equanimity brings in all virtues automatically, without the exertion of any effort on your part.

A few more thoughts before closing: If you find yourself in a situation where you cannot find equanimity amidst duality, take it as a learning opportunity. Do your best to identify what it is you are feeling and then to seek the opposite. If you are feeling angry, seek peace. If you are feeling sad, try to find a silver lining. If you are experiencing hatred for another person, do your best to identify something you admire about them. If you are feeling greedy, go out of your way to give graciously.

This neutralizes the negative thoughts and feelings you were experiencing.

Even though duality and equanimity may seem like abstract subjects, they wield major impact on our happiness. Acceptance of the present moment is not an easy attitude for an untrained mind. Yet while an unconditional acceptance of the present moment may feel like a loss of control, it is also a loss of attachment and judgment. When you accept the present moment, knowing that what is happening is supposed to be happening, and that what happens in the future is supposed to happen too, you will find yourself free from guilt, regret, confusion, apprehension, and fear. That is because the ultimate result of equanimity is peace. Equanimity gives you freedom from pain and suffering, allows you to exercise control over your own mind, and helps you to move beyond the extremes of duality.

Form a habit of watching your emotions at different times during the day. Observe your feelings. Are they positive? Negative? Are you feeling depressed? Do you find that you are feeling loving, angry, or jealous toward others? You must watch your feelings with the sole purpose of observation. Be careful not to pass any judgment on your emotions, or to react to them. Simply be aware of them until they disappear. Your awareness is the key. Don't be discouraged; even the most brilliant Olympic medalist was once a stumbling beginner.

Just like anything, achieving equanimity requires patience and practice. But believe me when I tell you that it can be done, and that the reward is well worth the effort.

Yours, in peace,

Purandar

Points to Remember

- Emotions by themselves are neither good nor bad.
- Know that your thinking and judgments create good or bad emotions.
- The combination of emotion and thought can be a deadly poison if negativity is involved.
- Be aware of your emotions.
- Beware your intensity, especially with negative feelings; the intensity of your emotions will cause an equal and opposite response in future.
- What is in the present will change; meditate on the temporary nature of present circumstances, relationships, and thoughts/emotions.
- Know that what you have will leave you sooner or later.
- The easiest way to achieve equanimity is to stop judging.
- You must know your struggles and battles to know and appreciate peace.
- Choose peace over everything, and everything will come to you.

My Notes

13

GLUE

August 27, 2014

Dear Uma,

Mountains allow the very dirt and rocks they are made of to move about freely. Birds abandon their empty nests when their chicks have grown. Trees shed their leaves without any hesitation. So why do we – humans – find it so hard to let things go?

There are several elements that make up you – Uma. The first element is your soul. The second is your ego. The third is your mental body, including your intelligence. The fourth is your emotional body. And, finally, there is your physical body. All these together make up that which is known as Uma. Your body is a representation of the ego's element of separation. The body, comprised of the Earth element, carries the magnetic properties of the Earth with it. These magnetic properties, in conjunction with the ego's other element, self-preservation, create attachment. This attachment is a form of energy that operates on a subtle level, making it unrecognizable to most people. Have you ever asked yourself who really owns your property? You might say, "*I* do. *I* own my property." Your physical ownership is recognized as belonging to your physical body. Your body is an instrument of your ego, used for identification purposes only. This means that, while your body is identified as the owner of the property, your ego will claim to be the owner and exert itself as such.

The energy of one's attachment is reflected in numerous ways; pride, accumulated wealth, possessions, etc. Since the mind is the bridge between body and ego, the issue of "mine and thine" comes in the play. The ego clings to your body's attachments and makes it difficult to let them go. Your attachments stick to you like glue. And, since attachment applies to nearly every aspect of your life – from possessions to relationships to ideals – they are particularly difficult to dislodge. You have an attachment to anything you think of as "mine." Again, this identification is the work of your ego.

One of the easiest ways to begin to address your attachments is by observing and establishing a separation between ego, mind, and body. First, you must view yourself as separate from your body. If you can separate yourself from your feelings of "mine," then you can observe your attachments as a neutral witness. When you witness your ego's sense of ownership, you can more objectively view the relationships between your body and your possessions, your acquaintances, your job, etc. Because you are now a neutral witness instead of an active participant, you can more clearly see the things that are troubling you in the various aspects of your life. At this point, your judgment is not clouded by the ego's efforts of self-preservation and separation. If you can detach in this manner, you will reduce your stress immediately. Remember, stress is an energy that is fed by emotion and attachment. When you remove the elements that are fueling your stress, it can no longer exist.

I asked you before to give up your viewpoints, concepts, beliefs, etc. You must do this in order to see objectively. If you can observe your circumstances, emotions, and thoughts dispassionately, then your stress will be gone. Remember that stress is born of emotional energy and cannot survive without attachment.

Another aspect of attachment is your memories. Your memories, and the energy that they carry, create emotions that tie you to them. Oftentimes, your memories will prevent you from releasing those emotions. The closer the memories are to your heart, the more difficult they are to let go. Even though it may be difficult for you to let release your memories now, if you do not, they will bring you more pain later on. Learn to detach yourself from these memories early on, and you will save yourself a lot of grief.

Pure emotions, such as love, joy, and peace, are the language of the heart, and offer feedback from your soul. Negative emotions, such as attachment, jealousy, or greed are properties of the ego. When you are trying to make a decision, attachment will cloud your judgment. If you want to make the best decision, free yourself from emotional influence, then detach yourself from any memories that might creep in to confuse the situation. Once you have detached yourself from these, you will be able to observe your issues objectively and it will be much easier to attain their resolution. You will view your situation as a third-party witness, aware of your emotions, but not influenced by them. Instead, your decisions will be based on wisdom. Know this: any decision you make that is followed by a feeling of peace, is a good decision.

The ego's hunger for control and ownership can even be seen in how you view obstacles or the problems you face in your life. Most people view problem as "theirs." You may have heard someone say, "This is my problem," or "It's my problem – I'll fix it." This is an example of the ego playing tricks by exploiting your attachments. Nothing is *your* problem; the challenges you face are a result of your attachment to your body. Again, if you can separate yourself from your body, you can view your issues objectively, free from attachment.

The emotional and mental benefits of detachment are enormous. When you can view yourself as separate from your body, it will be easier for you to remain calm and peaceful. Many people have a hard time realizing the benefits of this separation. Look at it this way: whatever issue you are facing, the situation is – at best – temporary. When you die, all bodily attachments will end; you cannot take anything you own with you once you have left your body. This includes your relationships, irrespective of blood ties, marriage bonds, job commitments, etc. Of course you can enjoy your possessions, but enjoy them as the temporary attachments that they are. You must not hold tightly to anything – not your house, your work, your car, or even your family. All this is temporary. It is wise to heed the words of Buddha, who said, "Meditate on the temporariness of everything."

Know this to be true: whatever issues you may have, know that there are many participants. These participants could be your spouse, your employees, your employer, your business associates or any other party you might encounter. Such parties carry either cooperating or opposing energies that, through the principle of resonance, affect you. Consequently, your own energies will be either strengthened or weakened.

That is why it is so important to cultivate positive energies, such as love and peace. They serve to protect and help you.

Imagining yourself as separate from your body is one of the most effective ways to get rid of your attachment to your body. Its effect will be like brain surgery. While you are imagining yourself being separate from your body, regard the empty vessel as you would an inanimate – even useless – object. Lay it aside, just as you would when you throw a piece of trash into the garbage. Walk away without fear, regret, or emotion. Make this as realistic as you possibly can.

You will immediately feel peace. This is freedom. Detaching yourself from the body (i.e., observing yourself separately from your body), even in your imagination, will bring substantial benefits. You will feel calmer, which will in turn project peace and calm toward those around you. Don't be surprised if your family relations grow more peaceful and harmonious. This is because detachment will pacify the negative energies that feed your problems. Your conflicts will become much more manageable because you will be able to seek a solution from a place of tranquility. By letting go, you will gain control of your emotions and your mind.

With peace,

Purandar

Exercise

Imagine that you are attending a funeral service. You make your way into the parlor, where a plain casket lies open at the front of the room. As you make your way to the casket, imagine that it is your lifeless body lying inside. Does the thought make you uneasy? If so, do the following exercise.

When you go to bed at tonight, lie on your back with your arms at your side, your hands facing downward. Do not cross your feet.

Take few deep breaths. Become aware of the energy circulating throughout your entire body. Shift your consciousness toward your heart center. Now imagine all your energy moving up toward your throat and the middle of your head. Finally, allow the energy to exit through the top of your head.

Imagine yourself standing outside of your body at the funeral service. Watch as your friends and relatives carry your body to the burial place or cremation grounds. Feel yourself released from all worldly troubles, worries, and pressures. Feel the freedom and peace.

Come back and enter into your body again as a free individual.

You may need to do this exercise several times until you are comfortable with leaving your body without emotions.

My Notes

14

JUMP

July 26, 2014

Dear Uma,

When you see leaves falling in autumn, know it as a unconditional surrender. When you hear the playful babbling of a brook as it flows down the mountainside, know its happiness in its surrender. When a flower lovingly gives its pollen to a passing bee, know the gift of its surrender. Likewise, when you surrender to the moment, you will know peace, happiness.

Since Western culture emphasizes the virtues of diligence, responsibility, and control, we tend to frown on the mere suggestion of surrender. Most people completely misunderstand the essence of the word. We have been so conditioned to resist all forms of surrender that the word itself is regarded with disdain. Surrender is often viewed as a weakness in our society, but this is not true. Surrender requires great courage and mental fortitude. It is about the hard work of being patient with yourself and your circumstances. Surrender does not mean you give up; it simply means you accept the present moment willingly, without judgment, so that you can move forward in peace.

When it comes to surrender, most people either have doubts or are inclined to resist it. Since no one person can know the entire breadth of any one situation, this resistance is based on imperfect conclusions. The root cause of our resistance comes from the failure of our expectations, based on such dualities as likes and dislikes, right or wrong judgments. It is only human to expect something. Everybody favors his own expectations while opposing the other side's competing interests. In this condition, it is likely that some expectations will not be satisfied. Such an event can bring joy and grief to different parties.

What I am attempting to get across is that our *viewpoint* is what determines whether something is bad or good, not the event itself. Our resistance to the situation is further agitated by the ego and its preferences. When you resist any situation, whether on a mental or a physical level, you will create friction and begin to build up conflictive emotional energy. Conflict destroys peace. It requires time and energy to pacify it. In addition to this negativity, your resistance will do nothing to change the situation. Despite what you may believe, you have no control over outside circumstances. However, by surrendering to the moment, you will, in turn, gain freedom from tumultuous emotions and find that you now have control over your mind.

Many think of surrender as a non-action. Not true. Surrender is the unconditional acceptance of an event, a person or a situation in the present moment without making a judgment of likes and dislikes or any other preferences or expectations. Surrender does not prohibit you from taking action; but it allows you to approach the situation from a clear state of calm, so you are free to take the best and most appropriate action in the next moment. If you remain detached, you will be spared from the ups and downs of your emotions. When you accept this way, you gain a major victory over the ego, because you are exercising control over your mind. You will have developed a precious element called equanimity.

How can you surrender to the moment when you are in fact resistant to the very idea of surrender? First be aware that in the present moment, each thing, event, or person exists as a matter of fact. And then know that there is also a resistance in your mind due to your preconceived notions as good or bad. Be aware of your emotions and reactions as an outside witness. Let yourself feel out your emotions while you observe them, but do not allow them to take you over. By doing this, you will release a great deal of emotional energy. Because you have dealt with your pent up negative energies, your mind will begin to experience calm. You can take action with a calm mind. Know this: when you resist, you lose.

Let's say that you have lost your job. If you view this as "bad" news (within the limits of your knowledge), there will be plenty of negative thoughts and fears of the future competing for your attention. But you must not allow them to fill your mind. The reality of the present moment is that you are no longer employed. You must accept this fact with a detached attitude. Surrender to the moment without judgment or expectation. Since you do not know the future, you cannot accurately predict how this situation will turn out. You may focus on the fact that you have lost your source of steady income, but this offers you the new opportunity to apply for an even better job or to strike out on your own. Your surrender will allow you to accept this event, without lessening your peace.

You might ask me how you could simply accept devastating events, such as the failure of an investment, the death of a spouse, or the loss of a job and telling you to surrender. However, if the loss has already occurred, then I might ask you, "What can you do to change what has already happened?" The more you fight against what you cannot change, the more grief you will cause yourself. How can that be possible? Remember that the more you resist (i.e. fight against) a situation, the more it persists, and the more negative energy you will build up. That negative energy can only bring you pain and suffering. Why follow such a destructive path, especially when it will not bring back what you have lost? Allow yourself to find peace, by accepting the present moment just as it is. Acceptance will free your mind from turmoil and will allow you to move forward with a sound mind.

Now consider the role of duality. The nature of duality requires that, in every situation, you have equal opposites of both sides. This means that the negative includes the positive, and vice versa. If you encounter something you perceive to be negative, the law of duality requires there to be an equal and opposite amount energy – i.e. positivity. The role of duality offers us the best argument for detachment: Since nothing can be completely good or completely bad, we can never fully understand what may come of any event; therefore, it is best to maintain equanimity (peace) by surrendering to the moment.

As discussed earlier, duality also appears in our likes and dislikes. This can cause further problems when these likes and dislikes compel us to create expectations. This goes on continuously in our daily lives: in traffic, during a phone call, when browsing your email inbox, with your relationships, when trying to make it to a meeting on time – you are always creating expectations.

Let's say, for example, that you are taking a flight for a business trip. You requested a window seat when you booked your ticket, so you expect to have the seat you prefer. But when you get to the airport and check your luggage, you find out you have been moved to a middle seat. Of course, you are disappointed. Your frame of mind in this moment will affect the entirety of your trip. If, because you did not get the seat you liked, you allow your disappointment to color your disposition, you may never discover that you are sitting between a syndicated journalist and a CDC scientist. Instead of conversing with these interesting people, you could easily spend the entire flight consumed by your own negative thoughts.

When you refrain from labeling things as good or bad, desirable or unwanted, positive or negative, you will gain peace of mind. With a calm mind, you will be better able to think clearly and decide wisely what the next course of action should be, without being weighed down by emotional baggage. Prejudices, preferences, opinions, mental conditioning, and past experiences are all contained within the memories of the person has them. The pre-conditioned mind has created so many likes, dislikes, and consequent expectations that the existence of such things is now considered a "normal" part of living. Most individuals remain completely unaware of these conditional ties. It is this unawareness that creates stressful living.

Can we change this mental setup? How difficult is it to change our notions, once we know that the source of our sorrows is within us? Let's view this scenario from a different vantage point. If you believe in God or the higher forces of the Universe, know that the will of such higher forces always prevails. If it is divine will, no matter what you do, you cannot succeed in stopping it. Your duty is to play the necessary and appropriate part. In addition to this, you have no way of knowing the complete plan of such higher divine powers. The perfect plan of divine will may seem imperfect to you, but in the long run, you may come to appreciate the situation as your view of its effect in your life changes. If you are an atheist, be aware that there are forces beyond your control. They may be financial, social, political, or indiscernible. You, as an intellectual person, need to adjust your mindset in accordance with the present; accept it wholeheartedly and move on.

It is vitally important that you change your thoughts and combat the conditioning of your mind. Don't bring the future into the present. Decide whether you want peace or struggles. Stop resisting and accept things as they are. Realize the temporariness of events, relationships, and possessions. Surrender to the moment and know peace. What I'm offering you is million dollar advice; don't take it lightly.

With peace,

Purandar

Points to Remember

- Surrender is the acceptance of what "It Is" in the present moment.

- Know that what is in the present moment is temporary; this too shall pass.

- Surrender is a call for action, not for reaction.

- Change is a continuous, natural occurrence- so is the present moment.

- There is no such thing as negative or positive, so remove these judgments (and classifications) from your mind.

- Our own likes and dislikes are the cause of our resistance and, ultimately, our stress.

Exercise

You may find it easiest to surrender when you are facing a particularly difficult situation. It is in these moments, when you are feeling compelled to fight back, that you will benefit most from surrender. This can happen when someone is insulting you, when you are feeling pressured by another person, or when you receive some unforeseen and seemingly negative news.

The next time you find yourself in one of these situations, check to see if you are feeling resistant. If you find yourself wanting to fight back or deny the reality of your situation, take a moment to practice surrender. Bring your awareness to your heart center. Remain there in a thoughtless condition until your body stops reacting.

Repeat this exercise again whenever your thoughts begin to linger on a stressful situation. The longer you remain in a thoughtless condition, the more successful you will become at surrendering to the moment.

My Notes

15

NO-FAULT INSURANCE

June 30, 2012

Dear Uma,

Everyone – no matter their race, religion, or beliefs – experiences things which cause them hurt. When something valuable is lost or an unpleasant event occurs, you will hurt. This hurt can manifest as seething rage, numbing shock, or crippling depression. Never is this fact more apparent than when we are hurt by another. The hurts that we inflict on each other can be the strongest and have the most lasting effects. While you may feel the need to blame the person you consider to be responsible for your hurt, nothing will help you more than to forgive them.

Hurt is both a mental and an emotional issue. Hurt is experienced by the ego, but its emotional effect is felt in the heart. Remember that the element of self-preservation and the element of separation are children of the ego. It is the ego's element of separation that causes our hurts. This process has a corrosive effect on your wellbeing. Hurt is a lower form of negative energy that affects you at a cellular level. Consequently, it can cause disease and weaken your body. Many times depression occurs. Deep-seated hurts can last lifetimes if not resolved quickly. It will percolate into the various aspects of your life, from your behavioral patterns to your interactions with others. If you do not want these hurts to continue to affect your life, then forgive.

Forgiveness must come from the heart, not the mind. Some people use mental exercises to help them forgive, such as repeating the phrase, "I forgive you." The underlying thesis in this exercise is that you consider the other party to be at fault, but are willing to let it go. This is a judgment, and an exercise at a mental level. These exercises are designed to impress upon the mind that there is no hurt. However, these exercises have a limited effect. They can only impress the need to forgive on the mind. But hurt is an emotional problem; its seat is in the heart. The emotional energy of the hurt must be released from the heart, and you must feel such release at the heart level. The exercise suggested hereafter should be done several times, until you feel light and happy. If you have released the hurt from the heart, you will feel relieved, light, or as if a burden has been lifted. A feeling of compassion will arise from forgiveness, and peace will follow.

One of the best ways to convince yourself to forgive is by recognizing that there is a greater plan at work. This plan is beyond our comprehension. Know that there are infinite causes in the scheme of creation that lead to any event, word, thought or situation. Such causes are beyond your control and the comprehension of all participants. Once you accept this, forgiveness becomes easy. The blame game is over. When Jesus was being crucified, he said, "Father, forgive them, for they do not know what they are doing." There is a lot of truth to be found in this message. First, know that everyone is experiencing hurt. When someone has hurt you, you must understand that their behavior was completely natural given their own level of consciousness and past experiences. When you judge them, you are doing so from your own limited perspective. Thus, two perspectives – your own and that of the other party – have collided, and disharmony is the result. Even though they may have intended to hurt you, such an action was the result of their own improper mental conditioning. By acknowledging this perspective, you will be able to understand the opposite side of the conflict, which will help you to forgive.

You must also realize that your own viewpoints and mental conditioning have limited your understanding of the situation, judgments, and perspectives. When you judge another's actions within your own limited perspective, disharmony occurs. Therefore, what you perceive to be the truth is only a half-truth at best. Once you accept that there are two sides to every story, you can let go of the erroneous notion that your side of the story is the "right" one. This self-righteous attitude creates certain expectations from the person or encounter. Failures of such expectations create the pain that you bury temporarily, but such buried pain remains deep within you, even while you attempt to forgive. The remnants of such buried pain can manifest again even under dissimilar circumstances and even with different persons. Let go your expectations and develop a sense of detachment toward the outcome, even before the encounter. Look at your hurt objectively, and you will see that your judgments are just as broken as the other person's. Understanding this perspective will help you forgive. Once you look at the hurt objectively, the process of healing becomes easier

Another approach is to release the need to have a specific outcome of words or deeds from the encounter or person. Such non-anticipation will set you free. Forgiveness may not be needed, irrespective of any outcome.

Finally, the energy of conflict or hurt can manifest in other forms. You may end up in conflicts with other persons. This energy can also impact the financial, employment, property, or health aspects of your life. I have seen these things happen many times in many people; lives. It can wreak incredible damage.

With peace,

Purandar

P.S. Know that forgiveness is an attitude of detachment from your own perspective and that you should adopt this attitude for the sake of your own peace. You are not doing a favor to someone else; you are relieving yourself from the burden of holding a grudge.

Exercises

If you are having trouble forgiving someone who has hurt you, go through the following exercises. Know that, at an energy level, there is no difference between what you imagine and what is made manifest. It is the energy that will bring the result.

Find a quiet place where you can sit undisturbed. Avoid any movement by your body. Take a few deep breaths. Hold each breath for a moment, and then release it slowly. Try to devote the same amount of time to inhaling, holding the breath, and exhaling. Do this until your mind is calm.

Feel the peace in your body. Bring your attention to your heart center. Concentrate avoiding any train of thought. Keep watching your breathing until you become thoughtless.

a. Bring the person you think is responsible for your hurt into your imagination. Now imagine yourself assuming the place of the person who hurt you. Realize that you would have done the same thing that the other person did to you if you had been in their position. Forgive (knowing that if you had the same amount of knowledge, wisdom, mental conditioning, and consciousness, you would have acted exactly the same way the other person has acted.).

Watch your body when you think of this hurt.

Observe the emotions you feel when you think of the hurt. Whatever you feel – whether rage or depression, betrayal or heartache – continue to feel the emotion, without thinking of the person who caused your hurt. Do not try to interpret or understand your emotions; just allow yourself to feel them without attachment or thought.

Observe your body as you continue to feel your emotions. Identify any particular part of your body where you are experiencing any kind of sensation. Again, do not try to interpret or understand these sensations. Just observe.

Now, imagine your body as a transparent shell, clear as glass. See the sensations and emotions you are experiencing as the energy that they are. Watch as this energy passes through your body. Now, see the energy being released from your body.

Once you feel that the emotions have passed through, seeing nothing left behind in your body, you should feel calm. Fill your body with pure white light. Let the light come into your body from every angle. Once your body is filled with the light, let the light pass out of your body, as you did with your emotional energy. Keep filling and emptying your body of the light until you have achieved complete tranquility.

Now, fill your body with pink and blue lights. (Pink and blue lights symbolize love and faith.) See these lights expanding in your body, filling it completely. Watch as the light expands beyond your body. See these lights transferred to the person who caused you hurt.

You can repeat this exercise again and again until you find that you have fully forgiven the one who has hurt you. At the end of this process, you should feel complete peace. The emotions and the memories of the event will no longer affect you.

<u>My Notes</u>

16

DIAMONDS OR ROCKS

April 20, 2014

Dear Uma,

What will be revealed in the next few paragraphs will open your eyes to the truth of emotional situations. Once you accept this truth, you will finally be able to relax.

Everybody experiences tumultuous emotions, such as anger, jealousy, greed, or other negative energies. These emotions form what Buddhists refer to as a "pain body." It is called this because resentment, hatred, self-pity, guilt, jealousy, depression, possessiveness, and even the slightest irritation are all forms of pain. These negative emotions carry their own energy frequencies and create their own living body of dim light – the pain body. As with any living thing, this body will attempt to create situations where it can feed itself with more pain.

Let us harvest peace from pain.

Energy does not differentiate. This means that when you experience discord in one area of your life, you may find that other areas of your life are also negatively affected. A prime example of this is divorce. Individuals who are undergoing a divorce will often find their relational discord spilling over into other areas of their lives. Their finances, their possessions, and even their other relationships will all be pulled into the fray. Look back on your own history for times when you faced a dire situation. Can you see how your buried feelings and suppressed energies brought calamity to other parts of your life? Resolve these feelings now, before they can cause you more harm. If you have trouble finding an example in your past, ask a trusted friend or partner to help bring to your attention anything you might have missed.

Most of us focus on the effect (pain) because we are not aware of the cause (Karma). Awareness, which is the only way to wipe out Karma, is the only way to combat the pain body. The key to becoming aware is to consider the pain as truly separate from you. Be aware of it, staying conscious of your thoughts and emotions, but do not give it the attention it craves. Know the feeling of your pain, but do not let the feeling turn into thinking. Sustained consciousness (without thinking) will sever the link between your pain body and your thought processes. Your awareness should be an independent witness.

Why does this work? Awareness is conscious, divine energy that disconnects cause and effect. It takes you in the present moment. In the present moment, there is no duality; nothing can exist. Therefore, cause and effect merge. When you are aware of the present moment without thinking, you are not analyzing the situation. If you are not analyzing, then you cannot judge anything as "good" or "bad" (i.e., the functions of duality). If you are simply aware in the present moment, then duality cannot survive. Therefore, becoming aware of your pain without feeding it will ultimately bring you peace. This is the process known as transmutation of energies.

If you have lived with the pain long enough, your efforts may be met with resistance. This is because you have formed an attachment to the pain. You may even have grown to like the pain, as it is familiar and close to your heart. If this is the case, observe your pain and identify the peculiar pleasure you find in being unhappy. What compels you to think of your pain? What emotions feed your pain? What behaviors indulge your pain? Observe your feelings of anger and jealousy. Identify your frustrations. Observe all these things without judging, analyzing, or identifying them as "yours." Observation is a wonderful spiritual practice; it is a medicine that will cure a multitude of diseases (i.e. attachment, anger, greed, jealousy, etc.).

How should you respond to such stressful situations? Your job is to remain quiet and peaceful. Once you realize that the problem is not yours, it is easier not to react. By remaining calm, not only are you doing yourself a favor, but you are doing a favor for the other person who caused you the pain as well. Later, when the other person has gone off and calmed down, he will look back on the situation and realize how calmly you responded, without anger or malice. You may even find him apologizing to you for their angry outburst. You will have, at least, saved yourself from further deterioration, and possibly have saved your relationship.

Emotional energy is extremely intense. It compels you – even forces you – to react. Anger, hate, jealousy, greed, and attachment are all emotions made up of negative energy. Emotions for sex are deadlier than anything else. When individuals attempt to suppress the negative energy that fuels their darker emotions, it is the same as pushing down a coiled spring; eventually, the energy will explode as the spring releases. Negative emotions can be expressed in many ways; every day we hear tales of rape, murder, and unspeakable brutality perpetrated across the globe. This is the result of suppressed negative energy exploding into physical expression. The saddest truth of this reality is that such devastating actions need not take place. There is a much better way to deal with negative energy.

When you are facing an emotionally charged situation, your first step should be to calm yourself down. Once you are calm, be aware of the emotions you are feeling. Observe any thoughts you might be having that are fueling your negative emotions. Once you have identified these thoughts, be sure not to indulge them. Remember that time is the vehicle of thought; therefore, the more time you spend thinking about something, the more energy it accumulates. Your goal is to stop any thought patterns that are feeding your negative emotions. Be aware of their presence, but do not spend your time actively thinking, analyzing or judging. Awareness will dissolve your thoughts since nothing can survive when exposed in awareness. At the same time, watch what your negative emotions are doing to your body. As you become aware, your emotions will become less forceful.

Now, let me ask you a few more questions: Does someone dislike you? Has someone criticized you wrongly? Has someone ignored or insulted you? Is someone angry at you? If your answer to any of these questions is, "Yes," then take a moment to think about how you react to such situations? If you reacted toward the other person in kind, showing anger, malice, or disdain, then it was you who truly lost the battle.

You must realize that this is the problem of the other person, not yours. It becomes your problem if you react in the same manner. When a person becomes angry, negative chemical reactions take place in the body. Their blood pressure sky-rockets, their brain capacity is reduced, and even the energy field around them becomes violent. This holds true for any emotional outburst that manifests as an insult, criticism, or verbal abuse. Therefore, it is the one who gives in to anger and acts on it that loses in the end. Whenever you are confronted with a negatively charged situation, remember to ask yourself, "Whose problem is this?"

If someone dislikes you, do not waste your time asking yourself why. Rather than trying to find weaknesses, flaws, or faults within yourself that might keep the other person from liking you, realize that their lack of love is their own problem – not yours. Instead, spend your time focusing on your positive qualities. Realize that you must love yourself as you are. (Here, I am talking about your inner-self, not your physical body.) Next, know that all human love is conditional and temporary. Humans love conditions such as beauty, intelligence, riches, style, etc. It is not real love. When a particular person does not like you, understand that their lack of love is based on some condition. The issue is with their condition, not with you.

If someone is criticizing you, and you are feeling hurt, know that it is your ego that is hurting. Rather than judging whether the criticism is right or wrong, realize that this criticism will diminish the size of your ego. As the ego can cause you innumerable problems, this criticism will actually help you more than it will hurt you. As you accept this truth, your feelings of hurt will also diminish. You should also recognize that any criticism you receive is only the limited opinion of the other person. It is an imperfect judgment based on their wrong preconceptions and conditioning. Finally, take a moment to observe your own thinking. It is entirely possible that your thoughts, words, or actions may have revealed an area that needs improvement. Embrace this opportunity to better yourself.

Let us take one step further. Who are our best teachers? I don't mean those that educate us in school, but those who educate us in life. They are the ones who we perceive to be the most difficult. We may even consider these individuals to be our enemies. Yet in the larger context of the universe, these are the people who have taken up the role of teachers to make the greatest impact on our lives. They illuminate our own faults, weaknesses, and biases not by sermons but by exposing themselves in worst possible manners through their interactions with us. Can you imagine their sacrifices? When they are angry, they are testing our ability to remain calm. When they criticize us, they are revealing an area where we need to improve. When they insult us, they are testing our inner strength to love them in adversity, or deflecting our ego.

You might be thinking that the world doesn't work this way. Believe me when I tell you that this is the only right way to exist for the good of yourself and others. The idea may be foreign to you; that is why we call it "reverse thinking." Your mind has been conditioned to operate in terms of "give and take," or "tit-for-tat." That is why it is so important to embrace these concepts and train your mind to reject emotional reactions. As you practice, you will begin to experience the immense benefits of equanimity.

You can start by doing something as simple as walking away from a confrontational situation. Take a glass of cold water. Water is full of soothing energies. It is hard to remain calm when your mind and emotions are on fire. But when this happens, do your best to allow yourself time to feel out your emotions in a quiet environment. You may find it helpful to jot down your thoughts and feelings on a piece of paper. Burn the paper and imagine your emotions fading away. Allow yourself to feel compassion for the other person, even if it appears as pity. Once you find compassion for the one you are in conflict with, you will know that you are on the right track.

In such difficult situations, practice watching yourself – your thoughts and emotions – rather than focusing on what the other person is doing. This will take your mind away from dwelling on the other person's anger or insults. Once you have readjusted your focus to your own reactions, you will find they will be diffused. Stop thinking. Bring your awareness to your heart center without thinking anything and you will remain calm. When you have achieved awareness of yourself, you will be the master of the situation. Watching your own body's reactions against perceived threats and insults is one of the most effective ways to break the hold of the egoistic mind.

All emotions are made up of energy. We feel them because they are connected to our hearts. Hurts of the heart are difficult to heal compared to physical hurts. While a broken bone may take weeks or months to heal, a broken heart can span across lifetimes. As we know, energy cannot be destroyed. But it can be converted or transformed. Persons who are very sensitive are more likely to experience some form of hurt. In order to move past these hurts, you must understand how to transform the negative energy of the hurt. All religions advocate forgiveness as a part of this process. Though we covered forgiveness earlier, I am inclined to repeat that merely uttering the words does not help. There must be an underlying foundational understanding, as well as compassion, in order to forgive and let go.

One of the most effective ways to develop such understanding is this: Imagine yourself standing in the other person's shoes. Imagine that your mental development, similar knowledge, and level of consciousness are all the same as the other person's. Under these circumstances, you would have acted in the exact same way. Developing this understanding is the first step to real forgiveness. If you can understand this truth at the heart level, you will experience feelings of compassion, which will lead you to forgiveness. Get rid of your negative emotions;

they are like poison. Negative emotions have created wars, mass murders, rapes, and countless other atrocities. Even many physical diseases have roots in negative emotions. Do not give in to negativity. Be loving and peaceful under all circumstances.

Thankfully, the story does not end with these negative emotions. According to the principle of duality, there is an equal amount of positive emotional energy available to balance negative emotional energy. This energy is found in love, joy, peace, happiness, and contentment. These emotions are your most powerful advocate against negativity, as they are the messengers of your soul. While negative emotions can be nature's way of pointing out areas where change or improvement is needed, positive emotions bring wellness and prosperity. Do your best to cultivate these positive emotions, as their positive energy will attract similar energy from the environment, benefiting you in every area of your life.

Love is a primary emotion. Peace is the other side of the coin. Joy is the result of both love and peace. It is impossible for one to exist without the other two, as all three are intertwined. Love, peace, and joy are a fundamental part of our being. They are capable of destroying all other negative energies (such as jealousy, hatred, anger, etc.).

Do not consider attachment or lust as love. Love is divine. Attachment or lust is human. Love is permanent. Attachment

–lust is temporary. Love is without conditions. Attachment-lust needs conditions. Love arises from soul. Attachment-lust arises from the mind. The place of love is the heart. Attachment-lust's place is the brain. Love is without jealousy. Attachment-lust produces jealousy. Love survives time and place. Attachment-lust requires time and space. Now you can easily differentiate between love and attachment-lust.

So how can you find this true, pure love? The vast majority of humanity does not experience this love. Of course there are rare occasions when true love can be glimpsed, but most of the time it is attachment or lust that is mislabeled as love. Forget about finding true love outside of yourself; remember that human love is full of conditions and limitations. Begin your search with self-introspection. Look for any negatives that you have associated with love, such as jealousy, hatred, anger, etc. These are negative expressions of love. They are signs of attachment or lust. Be observant of these enemies. Whenever such feelings arise, watch them without thinking or passing judgment. Be aware of these emotions and your body's physical reactions to them. The more you practice this awareness, the less such feelings will appear. As these negative feelings become less frequent, the feelings of true love in your heart center will begin to grow. As these true love feelings of love grow, the energy around you will start to change. You will begin to emit different vibrations, and – due to the magnetic properties of energy and creation – you will find that others who emit such positive vibrations are attracted to you. Their vibrations will draw them to you. You do not have to search them. Love has no gender bias. This approach is not a quick fix; much practice is needed to reverse your thinking. But don't lose hope. If you persevere, you will find this approach to be a permanent solution to your pain.

Wishing you love, joy, and peace,

Purandar

Points to Remember

- Anger is like acid in the veins.

- Anger, as well as any other negative emotion, is the problem of the angrier person; do not take on another person's problems by reacting to their negative emotions.

- When you are faced with a conflict where negative emotions are at play, take care to watch your own thoughts and emotions, not the other person's.

- Avoid thinking about your own negativities; just be aware of them, but don't think about them.

- Nobody can hurt you unless you allow them to.

- In order to receive love, you must cultivate love for yourself.

Exercise

When you are faced with negative emotions:

- Be aware of your emotions, but do not judge their contents
- Be aware of your body's reactions to these emotions
- Let the emotions run through your body without reacting to them

When you are in an emotional state, do not let your thoughts get the better of you; the more attention you devote to them, the stronger they will become.

If necessary, remove yourself from the situation. Excuse yourself to get a glass of water or to take a walk. Remember to keep watching your body's reactions.

If you are having negative feelings toward another person, bring them into your awareness, along with any faults, weaknesses, or motives you presume them to have. Now, see these faults, weaknesses, or motives in your own self. This is a difficult but very effective way to let go of the situation.

My Notes

17

YOUR MASTER KEY

December 24, 2014

Dear Uma,

Whether you believe in God, some other higher power, or nothing at all, most people agree that there is a living energy that inhabits the bodies of humans. It is evident that animals, birds, and vegetation are also housing living energy. In fact, there is nothing in the universe that is insentient. It is this sentient energy, which we will refer to hereafter as "the soul," that I will now attempt to explain.

Essentially, our existence is comprised of three layers: the ego, the mind, and the physical body. Beyond these elements there is something called "the soul" that allows the ego, the mind, and the physical body to continue functioning. You might say that the soul is the power source behind our existence.

The structure of creation is reflective, projecting copies of the original. The soul is a copy of God – the supreme, all-encompassing universal energy. Likewise, the ego is a copy of the soul. This pattern continues throughout creation, going from the subtle to the gross. That is why our physical body, which is more easily perceivable, is a copy of our mental body. This mental body is nothing more than a reflection of the ego. Since all these are lesser versions of the original, it stands to reason that the original has power over its copies. This means that the soul can control the ego. The ego controls the mind, and the mind controls the body. Understanding this power structure plays a vital role in many of the exercises and techniques you have found in these letters. Think of the soul as the CEO of your existence. If you are having problems with middle management (your mind, or your ego), then you go to the top of the power chain to find a resolution. And this is exactly what we will do.

Because the soul is a reflection of God, it retains all the powers of God – i.e., omnipresence, omnipotence, and omniscience. The soul also has all the properties of God, such as love, peace, joy, patience, equanimity, and so on. If God is all capable of doing anything at any time and any place, then such powers are also vested in the soul. If God is pure light, then the soul's form is also light. The reason for all this discussion about the soul is simple: As a resident of your body, you have a very powerful instrument within your reach. Light is the energy that we can harvest. I want you to reach out and use it for your benefit. Just as the sun's light cannot be restricted or contained, so is the soul's light. Not only does the soul offer you an unlimited source of love, peace, and joy, it also affords you the power to destroy hate, anger, and attachment. All positive energies flow from the soul, and all negative energies are no match for it.

When you affect a change in your life by harnessing the power of your soul, you will find the transition to be easy and the effects to be permanent. Such changes will be the natural results of being in contact with soul. On the same token, peace being a natural state of soul, jealousy, anger, attachment, greed, and likewise such other vices also cannot survive when you are in contact with your soul. For example, let's say that you want to quit smoking. With the help of your soul, your urge to smoke can vanish instantly and easily. You can feel as if you never had such a habit. And, best of all, this remedy is completely natural. With the help of the soul, all such transformations in your life will be as natural as breathing. At times, you may not even notice that such a change has taken place. Only later, when you are faced with a challenge in your life, you will find that you have an abundance of love, peace, and joy flowing from your soul that will allow you to deal with the obstacles.

So how can you achieve these incredible benefits? First, you must find the seat of your soul. The soul's seat is like its address; even though it is present in every part of the body, you must go to the seat to make contact with it. Though it is present in every part of the body, its "seat" is located in the space about two and a half-finger' width away to the right side of the physical heart knock. When you are invoking your soul, bring your awareness to the seat (near the heart center and to the right). Most people will fail at this task because of their lack of faith, persistence, and concentration. But don't give up! Intensity, one-pointedness, and reverence are the keys to unlocking this treasure. It is also called a witness as it is always aware every moment as to what is happening. It is aware of your thoughts; sincerity and all your needs so do not expect results with disingenuous approach. The soul's energy is living, intelligent, ever-conscious, and all-powerful.

While there are rare occasions where contact with the soul is both sudden and explosive, most people will find this to be a more gradual process. This measured exposure is actually a protective measure installed by nature that allows you to enjoy the full benefits of contact with your soul without being overcome. The soul's energy is like a trillion watts of raw power. Not everyone's body can sustain such incredible vitality. But, through gradual exposure, the very atoms of the body will begin to change, becoming more adept at handling such vibrant energy.

When you are first beginning to make contact with your soul, you may feel minor movements or thudding sensations at the back of your head or around your shoulders. You may perceive lights around your physical heart or other parts of the body. You might even experience raw energy passing through your body. Do not let such experiences break your concentration, stir your emotions, or lead your mind to wandering thoughts; this is a trap. Even if you find the experience to be enjoyable, remember that you are an objective observer. Don't allow your reactions to distract you. Though you will initially make contact through basic meditative practices, eventually you will be able to access your soul whenever you want.

Achieving contact with your soul is an extremely important practice. Why? Because the old adage is true: You are always influenced by the company you keep. If you keep the company of your soul, you will find your transition to stress-free living will be easy and effortless. All the virtues of God, of whom the soul is a reflection, can be inherited. If you are seeking love, peace, or joy, then love your soul, make peace with your soul, and enjoy your soul. If you wish to be free from worries and fears, if you want your relations to be harmonious, then you must spend time with your soul in meditation. Do this and you will find that your outer circumstance will change dramatically. The outer is a copy of the inner.

With peace,

Purandar

Exercise

Bring your awareness to the seat of your soul, which is located roughly Two and a half fingers to the right of your physical heart. While you are invoking your soul, maintain your concentration. You may experience various sensations, but do not allow them to distract you. Simply observe these sensations, without thought or enjoyment.

Most people have a problem with concentration, being constantly distracted by their thoughts. Start small, by committing yourself to 12 seconds of unbroken, singularly focused concentration on your soul. Concentration also requires bodily commitment; therefore, you should be able to remain completely still while performing this exercise. When you are able to maintain your concentration without interruption for 12 seconds, gradually work your way up to 60 seconds. Each time you practice this exercise, continue to increase the duration of your concentration until you are able to maintain it for 30 minutes or more.

When you have achieved absolute concentration for an extended period of time, ask yourself the question: Who am I (if not the body)? Concentrate on this question, waiting for the answer with patient focus. You may have to perform this exercise multiple times. Repeat the question to yourself every 10-15 minutes. Do this with persistence, patience, and faith.

<u>My Notes</u>

18

COPIES

January 5, 2015

Dear Uma,

As we discussed earlier, there are certain scientific principles that apply to creation. One of these is creation's reflective creation. Everything is a reflection of the previous element in descending order, moving from the subtle to the gross. Therefore, the original is the hardest to perceive while the copies become more obvious as the reflections continue outward. Take your body, for instance. Your body is solid and obvious while your mind is fluid and subtle. Your body is easier to perceive than your mind because it is a copy of your mind. That is why we say that the outer reflects the inner.

Think back to our discussion of the mind. Remember that your mind is nothing but a collection of thoughts and memories. All your opinions, judgments, and experiences are encompassed in your thoughts and memories. These thoughts and memories are mere "threads" of living energy (positive or negative) that carry their own magnetic properties. They have a life of their own, and "live" around your physical body. These "threads" are in the forms of light specks and have infinite capacities to express themselves in a variety of ways. In this equation, the brain is just an instrument – a piece of equipment that the mind utilizes to express itself in various ways.

Let us assume that you are experiencing a conflict with someone. Because of this situation, you have created an opinion about the other person in your mind. You have also formed an opinion about the events and persons that have led up to this situation. Now, understand that these opinions, which were formed because of your particular viewpoints, have created boundaries around that person and event. These boundaries have the magnetic properties of the thoughts that created them and, therefore, will attract similar energies in whatever form they may be (different situations, events, persons, thoughts, etc.). This vicious cycle can accumulate so much energy that it spills over into other areas of life, such as one's health or finances. This happens because conflict is an imbalance. It is no wonder that such conflict is a breeding ground for stress. How or when this stress will manifest (or reflect) in the physical world is unknown, but the reflective nature of creation alongside the law of Karma dictates that the cause (stress) will produce an effect.

Nature's laws operate and prevail precisely and without fail. Let's consider the following situation: Say you hold the opinion that your employer's company is limited in resources and not likely to grow any further. This opinion, which is based on your own preconceptions and limited knowledge, will attract like-kinds of energy to you. You may find that you are suddenly lacking resources or facing stagnation in your personal life. It can manifest itself in any aspect of life since energy does not differentiate. This principle applies to everyone regardless of their belief system, their opinion, their education, or their judgments. As a principle of nature, it is an inescapable truth of life and applies to all of creation.

I have noticed that almost all people hold a firm belief regarding one or another matter. Yet humanity is still well behind in understanding its own mind. Truthfully, many of these beliefs are the byproduct of group conditioning experienced at various points in life. For example, if a news program announces that the U.S. is experiencing a gasoline shortage, the vast majority of the public will believe it. This is group conditioning which promotes the mentality of scarcity on a mass level. This amalgamation of energy will manifest physically in one area or another on a national level. This group conditioning also serves to strengthen individual beliefs that consequentially play into our everyday interactions. These beliefs and your blind commitment to them can be highly dangerous to you. The stronger the belief, the harder to relinquish it. These preconceptions are like heavy chains around your body and soul, forming a rigid but invisible barrier that blocks out anything contradictory. You must shed your viewpoints, opinions, and judgments so that you can finally embark on the path of self-realization. Open your mind to everything. Realize that anything can happen and everything is possible. Know that the mind can be a valuable gold mine or a dangerous minefield. Drop your limiting mental conditions and prejudices for your own sake.

You are probably thinking that this is easier said than doing. And you're right; it is much easier to talk about these concepts than to adopt them into your being. However, it will be much easier to get yourself on the proper path once you understand the mechanics behind the practice. Remember that the entirety of creation is based upon the principle of duality – negative and positive, likes vs. dislikes, love and hate, scarcity and abundance, etc. These opposing polarities are present in every facet of creation. Let's go back to the group conditioning scenario where there is a shortage of gasoline. Consider this: If gasoline has become scarce, it is likely that oil companies will enjoy an abundance of revenues as a result. In every situation you face, realize that there is an equal amount of opposite energy that exists in the same moment.

When you are experiencing negative emotions, the first thing you should do is look for the opposite viewpoint in that moment. If you are experiencing anger, try to find peace. If you are experiencing sadness, find something to be glad about. If you dislike someone, try to find something about them that you can praise. If you are having trouble finding the opposite energy in a particular situation, try to change your negative viewpoint in another area of your life. Recall the previous example of a gasoline shortage. If you cannot find a positive aspect to a rise in gasoline prices, perhaps you can cultivate gratitude knowing that you have abundance financially that will make it possible for you to afford the price hike. Remember that your mind does not differentiate between situations on its own. What is important is that you identify and hold onto the positive elements rather than the negatives ones. Your person could be dumb, but handsome. He may be ugly, but noble hearted. You will find that it is easier to maintain the positive than it is to perpetuate the negative.

Our mind is so strictly conditioned that we cannot even begin to understand this connected energy when it is at work in our lives. If you immerse yourself in abundant thinking, you will find abundance in seemingly unrelated areas. Perhaps you will find an abundance of love. Perhaps you will find an abundance of health. Perhaps you will find an abundance of money. Many people subscribe to the idea that you have to give before you can get. The same is true when it comes to energy. Your mind and emotions create an invisible field of energy that surrounds your physical body. This invisible body is much more powerful than your physical body. Its energy is magnetic, so it will attract thoughts, persons, and events that carry the same type of energy around you. If you wish to attract positive energy of any kind, you must first find the positive energy within yourself, and fill your mind and emotions with it. Your invisible emotional body of energy will change slowly or rapidly depending on the intensity with which you are focusing on and emitting positive energy.

Many of us believe only in what we can see, touch, or experience for ourselves; they limit themselves to the physical world. If you would prefer to limit yourself in this way, then be my guest. But recognize that everything you can see or touch in the physical world is the physical result of a thought. It is because of this truth that we say the outer reflects the inner; the physical world is merely a manifestation of thought. I would challenge you to look to the source rather than the copy. Even if you have a hard time accepting this principle, I urge you to develop a habit of self-observation. As you continually observe your thoughts and emotions, you will come to realize that it is you – and the conditioning, beliefs, and judgments you hold on the inside – that matters.

Self-observation magnifies your weaknesses, reveals your habits, and highlights your thinking patterns. It shows you who you really are. And this approach is easy because it takes place in the privacy of your own mind. Because of the divine nature of the soul, once we are made aware of areas that need improvement, we are slowly prompted change. These changes will continue in magnitude as more weaknesses are revealed under continued observation. Try to write down your self-observations – your feelings and thoughts – on a daily basis. After six months, go back and read your very first entry; you will be amazed at how far you have come.

Some persons have a hard time finding their own faults because they fail to practice self-observation. My Guru once instructed me not to criticize anybody or anything for an entire month. Then, at the onset of the second month, I was told to write down my observations. This exercise gave me so much insight into the depth of my judgments and how criticizing the world around me had become an insidious habit. There was hardly any instance where I did not express my opinion. And yet, since my knowledge of any given person, thing, or situation was inherently flawed and incomplete, these opinions and judgments were essentially unjustifiable. It is easy to find the faults in others, but we often are blind to our own shortcomings.

When you find faults, weaknesses, etc. consider them as your own faults and weaknesses. Faults, weaknesses, insufficiencies, strengths, or virtues are our own judgmental boundaries. In case you are unable to recognize them as your weaknesses-faults etc., or you do not agree, at least keep aside your judgments. If you can refrain from passing judgment on another, you will find that compassion and forgiveness for that person will begin to come naturally.

Our lives are governed more strictly by the laws of nature than by the laws of man. Modern wisdom would have us believe only in what our five senses can perceive or experience. Yet creation is comprised of more than just the physical. The elements of subtlety, energy, resonance, reflection, and reaction cannot be seen, touched, or heard – they can only be experienced and identified spiritually. It is the reflection of these elements that manifests in the physical world, where we perceive them with our five senses. For example, a feeling of anger or love might be reflected on your face or in your voice, but it is experienced on an emotional level. This is outer reflecting inner. Similarly subtle is more powerful than the gross. Air is subtle but when it takes a form of tornado, we experience its power. We cannot see the words but we know their power to cause damage or healings. Pay the attention to your inner thoughts and emotions, and observe how they are reflected outward. As you continue to observe yourself and gain control over your inner elements, you will begin to find peace. As you continue to experience peace in your inner being, you will find that peace manifesting outwardly in your life. Have a wonderful self-discovery.

With peace,

Purandar

Points to Remember

- Your viewpoints, beliefs, and concepts create your reality.
- Your current external circumstances are an exact copy of your inner belief systems.
- Realize that your inner beliefs are blocking your progress.
- If you want positive results, create a positive image of the person or event you are struggling with.

Exercise

If you are having trouble finding the positive aspects of a person you are in conflict with, try this:

Find a quiet place where you can enter a meditative state. Bring the image of the person into your mind. Now, begin bringing any characteristic or behavior about them that you do not like into your awareness what you do not like in him, forming a mental list of faults or shortcomings.

Now, go through this list and realize that each item reflects one of your own weaknesses. Now begin noticing incidents of these weaknesses in your own personality. Being aware of such weaknesses a few times will bring in necessary changes. This is an easy medicine. This is the nature of reflective creation. You bring in different persons in your awareness to enlarge your personality area. Observation and awareness are all you need.

<u>My Notes</u>

19

BEING ONE

March 10, 2015

Dear Uma,

Meditation does not belong to any country, culture, or religion. Such renowned leaders as Buddha, Jesus, and Mohammad practiced meditation throughout their lives. Even if you are an atheist, there is room for meditation in your life. The benefits of meditation are many, ranging from the physical and mental to the spiritual. How fully you experience these benefits will be in direct proportion to the effort you put into the practice. One of the greatest benefits of meditation is a calm and controlled mind. When we are faced with extreme circumstances that is when we need a calm mind.

As with any exercise, there are some tips that are generally recommended for meditation. This first is to maintain the same time and location when practicing meditation. This is suggested for a couple of reasons. The first has to do with your body's biorhythms. Biorhythms are the body's various fundamental cycles that regulate memory, emotions, temperament, etc. By meditating at the same time each day, you will be integrating the practice into your body's biorhythmic sequences more effectively. The second reason has to do with vibrations. When you meditate in the same location, the positive vibrations that you emit will begin to fill the space around you. These positive vibrations will not only build up in your meditation spot, but within you as well. In addition, by maintaining the time and place of your meditation practice, you will be training your mind to concentrate, which will ultimately help you with meditating.

It is always important to relax your body and mind before meditating. You can do this by breathing deeply and releasing tension from your muscles. This is equivalent to stretching out your muscles before you exercise; it is a pre-conditioning that will help you achieve your best possible meditation. In the beginning you will find breathing and meditation are conjoined twins. Our thoughts are invariably connected with our breathing. At this introductory stage, just know that deep breathing will help to calm your mind. At more advanced stages of meditation, you will realize that breathing is an obstacle. Many times, those who are highly accomplished in their meditation will actually stop breathing.

The initial purpose of the meditation is to get you to concentrate; the ultimate outcome should be to go beyond the mind. To achieve sustained concentration, one has to maintain a focus on a single form or idea. The more abstract the idea, the more difficult it will be to avoid venturing off along a rabbit trail of thoughts, which breaks your meditation. That is why it is recommended that you begin meditating by concentrating on a single form or focal point. This could be the form of a particular deity, the body's heart center, a lamp or candle flame, etc. Some people prefer to focus on an object or a light form while others will begin their meditation with a chant that calms their mind. On the other hand, if you concentrate on a form, it will be much easier. Many people concentrate on the chakras or wheels of light located in different parts of the body. All of these practices will help you achieve concentration.

If you have a problem with stopping your thoughts, it may be best to begin your meditation with some breathing exercises. One of the most common breathing exercises is this: Count to four as you inhale, hold your breath for another count of four, then count to four as you exhale. If you can, wait to inhale again until another count of four passes. The rhythm or beat of the counting should be the same. Another technique is to concentrate on the present moment. While counting to eleven, be aware of the present moment (i.e., any sounds, the clothes you are wearing, room you are in, the furniture around you, your breathing patterns, etc., all in the present moment). As you concentrate on the present moment, you will find that your thoughts will recede.

What I have described previously in these letters is physical meditation. True meditation is spiritual. Physical meditation will produce a calming effect. However, without spiritual meditation, you will not get the benefits such as contentment, deep-seated happiness, detachment, or equanimity. Understand that by "spiritual" I do not mean religious; spiritual meditation will take you beyond your body and mind. By getting into a state of non-mind-ness, even for a few minutes, you will be rewarded with many benefits I just mentioned. Meditation requires patience and practice.

Because meditation deals with the mind, many practitioners struggle with invading thoughts. Because your thoughts are connected with your breath, it is very hard to stop thinking. Do not be discouraged; the battle is ongoing, but the war can be won. Even those who are accomplished in meditation struggle with "the thought problem." The only difference between them and the beginner is that the seasoned practitioner catches these rogue thoughts early on and stops them.

The beginner is more likely to be lost in a train of thoughts for a longer period of time before they realize what has happened. This happens because your subconscious mind carries forgotten or incomplete thoughts with it. When you calm your mind, these subconscious thoughts that were never completed or forgotten, will rise to the surface and attempt to fill up the empty space of the mind. These thoughts show the content of your mind. They come up to the surface- to get your attention as the current state of you mind is being emptied out, and there is a room for subsurface thoughts. All you can do when this happens is bring your mind back to its point of concentration (a deity, your heart center, a light, etc.).

You may also experience physical sensations when you calm your mind. If you suddenly experience an itching sensation, the need to cough, or pain in some part of the body, know that this is the mind's attempt to remain active. You must maintain your concentration and keep your body completely still; do not let thoughts or sensations interrupt your meditation. Another obstruction is sleep. When your mind is relaxed, you tend to fall asleep. If you are physically exhausted when you come to meditate, it is much more likely that you will doze off (sometimes without realizing it). This can happen if you are meditating at the end of the day or close to your bedtime. That is why meditation in the morning is recommended. In the morning, your body is rested, your mind is fresh, and the atmosphere around you is more likely to be quiet. Each of these things will make it easier for you to meditate.

Now, let's look at a step-by-step guide to practicing the meditation. You can make any changes you desire so that these steps better suit your beliefs.

1. Find a peaceful and quiet location where you can go to meditate, and time during which you won't be disturbed. (If you are a beginner, early morning is recommended since there will be less noise and your mind will be calm from sleep.)

2. Do not wear tight clothing. Sit in a comfortable position, whether on a chair or cross-legged on the floor. (If you are sitting on the floor, use a cushion that is 3-4 inches high to sit on and place your knees on the floor; this will help you to sit with good posture and proper alignment.) You must maintain good posture (a straight spine) while seated so that the energy in your body can move about freely. Also note that a hungry or over-fed stomach will not help.

3. Always invoke divine help before you begin meditating. The souls of disembodied beings are wandering all around us. A thoughtless, calm mind provides an opening through which these souls can enter into your mind. Invoking the divine by asking for protection can shield you from intruders.

4. Relax your body with deep breathing. Loosen your muscles. You should be inhaling, holding the breath,

and exhaling over equal amounts of time. Imagine that each inhale is energizing different parts of your body, and each exhale is releasing your tensions and impurities. If you would like, you may use prayers, mantras, or chants to help calm your mind. You may also light a lamp if you feel so inclined. I do not recommend burning incense while meditating, as it disturbs your perceptions of smell and hinder the calming of the mind. As you calm yourself, stop all movements

5. If you have a lamp or a candle, you can light it and concentrate on the steady flame. Continue to concentrate on the light until your eyes close. Keep the image of the lamp in your mind. Bring the image of flame to your heart. Move the image to different parts of your body, and then bring it back to your heart. Now imagine the light of the lamp spreading out from your heart in all directions. See this light fill your body, then spread beyond your body to your home, family, neighborhood, city, country, and the whole world. Next, bring the light back into your heart. Continue to concentrate on the flame. If it disappears, that is fine.

6. If you do not have a lamp, you can work with your heart center. Some concentrate on the area between the eyebrows or on the tip of the nose. The heart center area – the space located two-and-a-half-fingers' width to the right of your physical heart – is a much easier place

to concentrate since it is considered the seat of your soul. You may feel movements, throbbing sensations, or vibrations in this area during your meditation. If you feel movements or vibrations, allow them to spread across your body. Imagine a light residing in your heart center. Visualize its rays of light spreading throughout your body and beyond in all directions, into infinity. Imagine the lights in front of and behind your body merging into one; imagine the same for the lights on either side of the body. Remain in this state for as long as you can. Whatever you experience, do not form judgments; just observe. Bring the light back to your heart center and concentrate further. (It is better to have no expectations of any experience since such expectations can ruin your meditation.)

7. Imagine energy (light) surrounding your body from head to foot. This light is transparent and may be white, blue, pink, or violet; not earth tones such as brown or black. Feel it being pulled upward. See the light extend from the top of the head as far as you can imagine – all the way through the earth's atmosphere and beyond the stars. Imagine your body becoming transparent, made up of gold or silver rays of light. Imagine your light merge with the light in the space around you. Become one with the light. Stay like this for as long as you can. Slowly begin to bring the light back. While

bringing back this light back from infinity, touch the stars; imagine their lights connecting with your light. As the light is brought back in through the top of your head, allow it to descend from the top of your head down through your spine and into the Earth. After some practice, you will feel electricity moving through every orifice of your body.

8. Bring the light back to your heart center. Stay as long as you can in this illuminated and thoughtless state. Slowly bring your awareness back into the world around you.

Meditation is a continuous lifetime journey. If you have practiced it in your previous lives, you will start from where you ended last time. I once knew an office janitor from Mexico who started to float in the air during his very first meditation. Do not be discouraged. Remember that this is a journey; enjoy it.

With peace,

Purandar

My Notes

20

THE INFINITE OCEAN

July 14 2015

Dear Uma,

When a river finally reaches its end, it faces an infinite ocean – an ocean of love. It accepts the river with all its faults (i.e., dirt, chemicals, debris, and so on). The ocean presents no conditions upon its acceptance. In fact, the ocean does not have a choice; it accepts the river as it was meant to. The river, likewise, does not mind losing itself completely, and offers itself to the ocean without conditions. It is an absolute merger of love.

When everything else – including all the advice in these letters – fails, love is the ultimate solution. You might ask, "What does love have to do with my stress?" The answer is, "Plenty." Have you ever felt all your problems melt away when you are greeted with a smile on the face of your beloved? Love has the power to overcome anything. So far, I have showered you with all kinds of advice, and discussions that have sometimes carried the intensity of a thunderstorm. But when we face the ocean, words fail us, and we become silent. All my advice can be summed in one word: love.

Having said this, it is important to realize that almost everyone will fail the true test of love. In today's world, we use the word "love" to describe a number of things. But, it is most likely that your definition of the word fails to encompass the true nature of love. This is partially because a precise definition of love is not possible. Sometimes, it is easier to start with what something isn't than to try to define what something is. So let's begin with what love is not:

- If you have a condition in a relationship, it is not love.
- If you have an expectation in doing something, it is not love.
- If you want somebody to conform to your views, it is not love.
- If you are hesitant to give up something or somebody, it is not love.
- If you are harboring jealousy, hatred, or annoyance, it is not love.
- If you differentiate for any reason, it is not love.
- If you judge something or someone, it is not love.

The list could go on forever. Many people confuse these things for true love, but they are actually a distortion of love. When you impose conditions in a relationship, they are often born of your attachments to things such as beauty, money, security, time, intelligence, etc. When you carry expectations for someone else, you are not loving them as they are. If, for example, you expect someone to conform to your viewpoints, this means that you consider your beliefs to be more valuable than your relationship. When you are differentiating (i.e., your ego is invoking the "mine and thine" mentality), you are attempting to exert ownership. While each of these examples shows a failure to achieve true love, that does not mean that love is not present or at work.

The first thing you must understand is that love is the source of everything – yes, including your stress and worries. Love is, in a sense, the mother energy from which all other energy flows. It is at the core of everything we know – from our thoughts and perceptions to our relationships and possessions. Emotions such as jealousy, hatred, and annoyance are negative forms of love. When you "love" something or someone, it is your fear of losing it or them that consequently causes you stress or worry.

Often times, the absence of something will show the presence of something else. For example, jealousy is a negative form of love that is present when you are lacking for something you desire. If another person is lacking a quality you would wish them to have, then you will find annoyance or even hatred is present. If you lack peace when you think about the people or things in your life, you may find the presence of fear and attachment. If you are not satisfied or content with your life, you may be comparing between your life and another's.

As love is the ultimate source of all energy, it expresses itself in infinite ways. Duality promises that whenever you experience negative energy, there is positive energy also though it may be hidden. Therefore, no matter what negativities you face, there is love to be found when you look beneath the surface. For example, there is an element love hiding behind jealousy. In anger, you will find love for either being right or something you love that you are not finding in other. In greed, you will see love for money or some other material things. Now if you do not care for these subtle differences, God may help you, but my point is well served. These subtleties show that love is the basic structural energy of everything that your eyes can see, your mind can perceive, your intelligence can grasp, and your emotions can feel. The more desperately you cling to your perceptions and beliefs, the harder this task will be. However, you must find the positive aspects in every problem or negative situation in order to be at peace. Remember that love and peace are two sides of the same coin; if you can find love, you will also find peace.

I am not naïve enough to suggest that your problems will immediately vanish as if they were wiped away with the flick of a magic wand. While love is the greatest solution, it is also an extremely hard taskmaster. Sometimes, it mercilessly crucifies you until you are forced to face the truth of a situation or problem. For example, if you find yourself unable to pay your bills, it may be love revealing the need for you to make drastic changes in various aspects of your life. Love will often present us with the opportunity to make necessary changes by forcing us into situations or events that are seemingly adverse. Many times, the lesson you must learn is hidden away in the deep recesses of your mind. While the reason may not be immediately apparent to you, love has a purpose in everything. Therefore, if you refuse to change your superficial view of the problem, it will remain. This truth can be hard to swallow, especially if you have very hardened viewpoints.

Having stated that love is at the core of every thought, word, and action – be it positive or negative – the real question becomes, "How can love be the solution of my problems when it is the root cause of my suffering?" All you have to do is to search for the positive effects of your suffering. Ignore the so-called negative effects and concentrate on the positive. If you can learn to identify the positive in any situation and cultivate love, your stress will go away. Here are some examples that might help you find love in adversity:

- Love in an accident: Be patient with yourself, be considerate of others, and observe your own behavior.

- Love in the loss of your job: Consider what new opportunities might be awaiting you – in acquiring new skills, meeting new people, making new contacts, and traveling to new places in life.

- Love in the loss of your reputation: Allow the situation to diminish your ego and realize the temporariness of everything.

- Love in the loss of money: Recognize the fleeting nature of wealth, and see the value in the present moment.

- Love in the loss of a relationship: Allow the person's absence to increase your appreciation for the value of that individual, while at the same time allowing them to be free from your shadow.

- Love in the loss of support: Seize this opportunity to be independent and walk in freedom so that you can recognize and appreciate your true value.

- Love in bills to pay: Let go of unnecessary possessions, change your priorities, rearrange your financial structure, and look for new resources. (This time-sensitive issue is really a compulsive force of nature urging you to look over your life from a new perspective.)

- Love in sickness: Reevaluate your life and forgive yourself for your mistakes, grudges, and hurts. It forces you to appreciate the value of a well-operating body.

- Love in death: Celebrate that this person is now free from bondage, attachment, worldly problems while you continue to appreciate the impact they had on your life.

- Love in your broken heart: Use this opportunity to differentiate between love and attachment or lust. Honor your true feelings. Experience love in letting go.

- Love in the uncertain future: Be patient with time and yourself. Know that the old has not passed and the new has not arrived yet.

- Love in legal battles (such as lawsuits or divorce): Appreciate the value of peace in stressful situations. Recognize the mistakes and avoid further conflict. Forgive the other person, knowing that this forgiveness is not for others, but for your sake.

I realize that actually carrying out these suggestions in the midst of stressful and sometimes devastating circumstances is easier said than done. Yet when you succeed in finding the positives within the negative, you will find love and the solution to all your problems. How is this possible? Because love is the requirement of peace. Have you ever seen peace in the absence of love? Peace cannot exist in stressful situations if you cannot cultivate love. In all difficult situations, you need first to recognize the root cause of the problem. Then, focus on the positive outcomes, rather than the negative effects. Again, this requires you to reverse your thinking. You will find, however, that focusing on the positive will calm you down immediately. Let peace encompass your being. It will provide you with a calm mind so you can think clearly on your next course of action. Whatever action is justified in the present moment – not worrying about its future outcome provides the support for the action that must be taken.

Now let's talk about something beyond logic. Have you ever seen love in a concrete physical form? No. But you have experienced it many times before. The energy of that experience has a three-pronged structure: resonance, reflection, and reaction. Resonance is a reverberation; it is an echoing effect. Reflection is the mirror image; it produces a copy. Reaction is the response from receiving the echo back; it is the result, i.e. Love for love. Peace for peace. When you express love – toward a person, problem, or thing – you release positive vibrations that spread outwards to the focus of your love. These vibrations are created by reflection. The object of your expression also releases vibrations. Resonance brings your vibrations into sync with any similar vibrations being reflected from the intended object. If your intended object or problem continues to generate negative vibrations, your positive vibrations will neutralize them.

If the focus of your love is a person, they will feel peace as a result of the positive vibrations you are sending to them (whether or not they know that you are the source). If you keep repeating this process, negativity will be neutralized and will ultimately turn into positivity. Positivity will make it easier to solve whatever challenge you are facing. This practice takes time, intention, intensity, and faith (though intensity can affect the timeframe and the quality of resolution). Here is a little caution: Doubt and expectations are your greatest obstacles to success. Doubt, which is the absence of faith, will weaken the force of your positive vibrations. Likewise, if you send love along with your expectations of a particular result, then you are actually sending a condition, which is not love at all. Your condition will fuel the conflict, not contribute to a solution. When you send true love to a person, problem, or object, it can only be without a condition or an expectation of a result. This means that you cannot hold onto any grudges, resentments, irritations, or hurts. You must also reject any notions of anger or revenge. Remember: Love does not allow for judgments. You can either hold onto your negative emotions and be unhappy, or let love flow from you and find peace.

A question arises in reverse: If you can project energies to other people, situations, and objects can they likewise project their energies onto you? The answer is yes; the principle also works the other way around. So how can you protect yourself from any negative vibrations that are coming your way? The first step is to practice awareness. As you watch your own thoughts and feelings, take note of negative feelings or thoughts about the person, situation, or object that repeat in your mind. If you find that you have such feelings or thoughts, then you are most likely on the receiving end of projected negative vibrations. Another way to become aware of outside negative vibrations is to go through a simple exercise. First, clear your mind of all thoughts and feelings. After a few seconds of resting with a quiet, thoughtless mind, bring the image of the person, situation, or object into your awareness. Without thinking, watch your feelings. Observe your body and how it reacts. If you feel uncomfortable, or your body jerks or shivers, it is time to take positive action on your part. When you are on the receiving end of negative vibrations, your own vibrations of love and peace will act as a protective cover.

Let me make one final point: It is light that carries the energy of creation. Did you know that the sun of our solar system is ninety-three million miles away from us? Do you think the Earth could survive without the sun? Yet the only connection between the Earth and the sun is light. It is the light of the sun that brings us the energy we need to survive on Earth. Have you ever seen light create a rainbow of colors as it passes through a prism? Did you know that various experiments have proven that these colors have individual and unique properties? For example, red light carries active energy and is also associated with anger. White light – or pure light – is associated with purity and peace. Blue light promotes spirituality, and pink light carries love. Therefore, when you are sending love, see it as a cloud of energy filled with pink light. If you want to protect yourself from negative influences, cover yourself with the pure and loving energies of white and pink light. Though this may seem like an imaginative exercise, remember that everything you see was first a thought in the imagination

If you want to find peace, if you want to find freedom, if you want to live without the weight of stress, anger, and resentment, then look to love. Only love can demolish barriers, calm tumultuous emotions, and bring an ocean of peace. Only love can defeat negativity, tranquilize your adversaries, and remove your stress. Love in action brings forth your best efforts in your duties, protects you physically and mentally, and gives you satisfaction in your being. Love is the solution.

I have rested my case for love. May eternal peace accompany you at all times.

Resting in love,

Purandar

My Notes

21

ALL IS WELL

July 22, 2015

Dear Uma,

Having crossed a tumultuous river of concepts, we have finally arrived on the shore. There have been many tests and battles, both within and around you. Although you undoubtedly failed a test or two and lost some of the battles, yet in the end, you have achieved the momentous victory of peace. You now know equanimity, and your natural state reflects the saying, "All is well." This peace has become like a blanket covering everything in your life. While conflicts and contradictions are a necessary part of life that helps you to value peace, you now know that all will be resolved in peace. The hard ice of your judgments, your beliefs, and your conditioning has melted; your mind has become a beautiful, flowing river.

Let me take a moment to affirm what you have achieved and learned:

- Your ocean of churning emotions is now calm and full of love.
- You observe all and refuse to react.
- You are surrendered to the present moment, accepting what is as it is.
- You act from this surrender, moving forward with resolve and clarity.
- You know that events the present moment are ever-changing, and, therefore, accept that your current judgments are also temporary.
- Your next actions will be in line with the next moment and without expectations.
- You understand that "right" and "wrong" are just subjective conditions that will change as time goes by; therefore, you never insist on being right.
- You have made a habit of observing your own emotions (jealousy, greediness, anger, attachment, etc.), and recognize them as temporary displays of the energies in the emotional body. You let these emotions go in your pure awareness.

- You observe persons and events around you, interacting with them as a normal human being, but internally knowing you are playing your part.
- Your inner peace now affects the people and events that surround you.
- Your inner peace attracts people and events that are peaceful and loving.
- You let the river of life flow effortlessly, enjoying its twists and turns and without being drowned in it.
- You have peace in the present; you have peace in waiting.
- You know that the ego has taken control of you when doubt persists.

Finally, you know all is well because there is something beyond your body that is omnipresent, omnipotent, and omniscient that takes care of your needs (but not your wants) and forces change upon you when it is needed.

We now know that Baboo worked for a cause, not for applause. He endeavored not to impress, but to express. His life illustrated how absence is more powerful than presence.

We now know that the elderly woman – my mother – who personified peace in turmoil, happiness in adversity, and strength in silence was living more richly than anyone else. These two showed all of us what life truly about – peace.

Uma, dear, I will reveal one more truth to you: The day that you entered my life, it was as a student seeking to learn spiritual lessons from my life experiences. Yet, unbeknownst to both of us, you also became a teacher to me. What a perfect contradiction existing within the same time and space. Today, I have finished my instructions. I have given you all of my wisdom – the most precious of jewels that I earned by struggling through many of life's battles. It was a lonely journey, but it will not be so for you. Your battles will make you spiritually rich, and will continue to bring you riches as time passes in this lifetime and those that are to come. It is my greatest hope that these letters will serve as a guide and an encouragement as you continue on your journey of reverse thinking and self-realization. A quantum leap is possible.

Let me depart now. We cannot stay as water forever; we must float away as clouds in the heavens.

In peace,

Purandar

<u>My Notes</u>

PARTING WORDS

Dear Readers,

It is said that the human mind remembers only 10% what it read just ten days ago. This concepted presented in this book may prove difficult to digest and challenging to practice for most people. Yet at the risk of being redundant, I am asking you to commit to performing two or three of the following exercises for just a few days.

- Practice Silence: Set aside one day a week (or at least few hours on the weekend) to practice silence. Keep your mind empty during this period.

- Cease from Judgment: If you cannot silence your mind for a day, try withholding criticism or judgment for one day out of the week. If there is a particular event or person that you think you may be critical of, try to withhold judgment and criticism when interacting with them or thinking about them.

- Accept What Is: For one day out of the week, do your best to accept whatever comes to you, without likes or dislikes.

- Refuse Anger: Each day, if you are confronted with anger (whether it be your own anger or someone else's), refuse to respond to it.

- Check Your Needs: Before going to sleep, look back on the day to check whether your true needs (not wants) were met or not.

- Forgive: Before going to sleep, forgive someone who insulted you or did not treat you appropriately. Then, ask forgiveness from whom you have hurt or treated unfairly.

- Decline the Negative: Refuse to watch, listen to, or participate in anything that is violent, and spurn criticism of all kinds; this includes television shows, movies, video games, music, etc.

- Watch Your Emotions: Observe your emotions or feelings three times a day.

- Send Love: Send your heartfelt love and gratitude to your enemies or any persons you are in conflict with, grateful because they are revealing your weaknesses to you; do this daily.

- Focus on Your Heart Center: Finally, when everything seems to fail, bring your attention to your heart center several times a day. Stay there for at least a minute (or for as long as you can) without any thought.

If you find these exercises to be beneficial, I urge you to continue. Do not attempt to practice everything at once; it is much easier to do two or three exercises for a sustained period. Rest will be added automatically.

A final word: When all is lost, and darkness surrounds you, know that the stars are still twinkling beyond the darkness of the night. The night is the mother of the morning; it is nature's inevitability that the sun will shine, birds will fly, rivers will flow, and flowers will bloom again and again. Human effort will continue with renewed hope and vigor. Know that every icicle in the winter, every sea breeze in the summer, every drop of morning dew has its time and place, and a function to accomplish; it is an infinite certainty. You have paid your dues – it is your morning to wake-up and rise again. A new dawn is already on the horizon. Time is moving on. My dear, it is your time to cross over to a new frontier.

In peace with you,

Purandar

AUTHOR

Purandar A. Amin, Attorney, Chartered Accountant and a real estate investor, whose lifelong interest from early childhood to present is a quest personified for the absolute truth. As a real estate investor, he authored "Foreclosures: How to prevent, stop, Beat and survive". His second book was a compilation of letters from a father to a daughter on her wedding day titled "River Flows, Letters to Rhutu". Starting from the very humble conditions to doing millions of dollars of real estate transactions, he experienced his life from many peaks and valleys, interacting with thousands of persons giving him a vast panoramic experience of the human life that is like a river that comes down from the mountain top, flows around obstacles and reaches to ultimate destination merging with its beloved. ". Now here comes the presentation of lifelong spiritual expedition -"Fearless Thinking, Stress-free living- Guaranteed (Almost). A Life Changing solution for Peace and Happiness". Enjoy the journey.

Contacts us:

Website: www.stress-freeliving.net

Facebook: www.facebook.com/DivineReflections101

Twitter: @DivineMind101

Instagram: www.instagram.com/DivineReflections101/

Thank you for spending few moments of your time with me. If you found this book helpful, Please let your friends know about it. If it turns out to make a difference in his life at a critical junction in the life, he will be eternally grateful to you.

If you have a few moments for me, please leave a short review on Amazon product page, on my web site and other review sites.

If you have questions as to the contents of the book, please use our website Q@A page.

www.ingramcontent.com/pod-product-compliance
Lightning Source LLC
LaVergne TN
LVHW051624080426
835511LV00016B/2158